Iceland

Front cover: view from the
Perlan, Reykjavík

Right: an Icelandic puffin

Þórsmörk • One of Iceland's most dramatic wilderness areas *(page 50)*

Reykjavík • Iceland's vibrant capital has many cultural attractions *(page 25)*

Geysir • No visit is complete without seeing this erupting hot spring *(page 44)*

Heimaey • A quintessential Icelandic fishing port with an attractive harbour *(page 47)*

Goðafoss • Witness the power of these staggering falls (*page 67*)

Northern Lights • The most breathtaking lightshow on earth (*page 14*)

Blue Lagoon • Bathe in the naturally heated, therapeutic waters (*page 39*)

Whale-watching • Spot one of these majestic creatures off Húsavík (*page 63*)

Lake Mývatn • A walker's paradise surrounded by volcanic peaks (*page 68*)

Jökulsárlón • This spectacular iceberg-studded lagoon is out of this world (*page 55*)

A PERFECT DAY

9.30am Big breakfast

Start the day with breakfast at your hotel or head to the retro-style café, Grái Kötturinn, on Hverfisgata 16, for orange juice, pancakes with bacon and syrup and plenty of coffee refills.

1.30pm Traditional Reykjavík

Take a walk through Austurvöllur Square, the city's traditional heart, where at the centre you'll find the statue of Jón Sigurðsson, Parliament House and adjacent, Reykjavík's oldest church, the Dómkirkjan.

12.30pm Fishy stop

Stop for a bowl of lobster soup and a beer at Sægreifinn fish shack on Geirsgata 8.

2.00pm Heritage walk

Walk down Reykjavík's oldest street Aðalstræti and look in at the city's most modern heritage museum, Reykjavík 871±2 Settlement Exhibition for some Icelandic history, then stroll along the banks of Tjörnin pond to see the abundant birdlife on the shore.

11.00am Shoreline stroll

Take a morning walk and head down to the shoreline and the harbour area. If you're tempted you could take in a whale-watching trip from one of the boats moored here. Check out Icelandic pop art at the Harbour House Museum and admire Mt Esja from across the bay.

IN REYKJAVÍK

5.00pm Steam and soak

Time to recover from shopping and sightseeing at Sundhöllin geothermal pool at Barónsstigur. Join the locals and indulge in an outdoor hot pot soak, or swim a few leisurely lengths in the indoor pool. The perfect way to get ready for the night ahead.

10.00pm On the town

Start with cocktails at the 101 Bar at Hverfisgata 10, then head off to Laugavegur, for a spot of nightclub-hopping. There are a number of trendy bars and clubs such as Boston (Laugavegur 28b) and Café Óliver (20a). Grab a hotdog *(pylsur)* with mustard from an all-night food stand on the way back to your hotel.

3.00pm Retail therapy

Head to Reykjavík's main shopping street, Laugavegur. The place is jam-packed with vintage clothes (Spútnik at 28b) and vinyl (Bad Taste at 28), along with exclusive, cutting edge fashion labels. An excellent place to stop for a coffee.

8.00pm Fine dining

There are many excellent restaurants in the city centre, two options for fine dining are along Austurstræti; Apotek Bar-Grill (at 16) housed in the old pharmacy or La Primavera (at 9) for a taste of northern Italian cuisine.

CONTENTS

27

64

80

76

62

11

INTRODUCTION

Few places on earth can match the raw and intense beauty of Iceland. Both fiery and cold, forbidding and inviting, it is a place of dramatic contrasts, home to immense ice fields, bubbling mud pools, colossal waterfalls and hot springs. Although Iceland has a long, rich cultural history, it is the land itself, sculpted by the forces of nature into a unique, ever-changing landscape, that tells the country's true story.

Underground Drama

In geological terms, Iceland is a mere baby, composed of some of the youngest rocks on earth and still being formed. Over the centuries, eruptions have spewed vast fields of lava across the island's surface and projected choking clouds of ash high into the air, blocking out the sunlight and blighting crops. In 2010, the ash cloud from a volcanic eruption under Eyjafjallajökull glacier paralysed most of Europe's air traffic for several days. Every day there are thousands of minor earthquakes and shocks, most of which are only detectable by seismologists.

The presence of so much natural energy just below ground makes it possible not just to see the awesome power of nature, but to feel, hear and smell it. The limitless reserves of geothermal energy that have produced such a varied terrain also supply heat and power to Iceland's homes, and the 'rot-

Plates apart

Iceland straddles the North Atlantic Ridge where two of the tectonic plates making up the Earth's surface are slowly drifting apart. The country is widening at a rate of roughly 2cm (¾in) annually. Along this fault line, from the northeast to the southwest, earthquakes and volcanic activity are commonplace.

ten egg' smell of sulphur is unmistakable. Dams across fast-flowing glacial rivers provide the nation with more than enough hydroelectrically generated power to meet its needs.

The abundant hot water not only heats homes and offices, in winter it is piped under pavements in the centre of Reykjavík to melt away the snow and ice. All year round it contributes to the social life of the Icelanders, filling outdoor swimming pools, where people meet to take a little exercise or just to chat in the hot tubs and steam rooms.

Pollution-Free Land

For Icelanders, keeping their landscape clean and pollution-free is a top priority. It's with justifiable pride that they boast that the water from any stream or non-glacial river is drinkable, due to the lack of heavy industry. Even in the capital, Reykjavík, the air is bitingly clean. You won't see rubbish tipped at the wayside here, nor will you encounter widespread burning of fossil fuels. The government has attempted to attract new heavy industry such as aluminum smelting, which needs high amounts of energy; however, the environmental impact of the new dam has roused huge controversy.

The Icelandic Horse

Horses have been used for transport and farming in Iceland for over 1,000 years. The country's isolation and a ban on importing new horses to keep out disease means that its horse population is remarkably pure. Icelandic horses are relatively small but extremely tough and they can handle the rugged terrain with ease. They are found in a wide variety of colours and are respected worldwide for their intelligence, stamina and speed. The Icelandic horse has a unique gait, known as a *tölt* – a kind of running walk with a gentle flowing movement that makes for a very smooth and comfortable ride.

Icelandic horses thrive in rugged terrain

High Standard of Living

Iceland is a European nation, although it remains outside the European Union mainly to protect its economically vital fishing grounds. It has strong social institutions and a well-funded welfare system. Few Icelanders are conspicuously rich, but there's little urban poverty, and the standard of living throughout the country is high.

Geographically equal in size to England, Iceland has only approximately 320,000 inhabitants, one third of whom live in and around the capital. Icelanders have a powerful respect for nature and know they can never expect to control it or have it all to themselves. The shy Arctic fox and the reindeer are rarely seen, but sheep are plentiful, and horses are widely kept. Millions of seabirds flock to the country's cliff tops and coastal meadows to nest during the bright summer months, while offshore, whales, dolphins and seals are abundant in some of the cleanest waters on earth.

Making friends on a farm

Icelanders make the most of the many benefits of their extraordinary environment, spending as much time as possible outdoors, weather-permitting. Walking, climbing and horseriding are popular pursuits, and, as the importance of tourism has grown, so too has the number of companies offering snowmobiling on the glaciers, hiking adventures in the interior and whale-watching off the coast.

Reykjavík

Dominated by brightly painted buildings and a massive central church, Reykjavík is a lively place. Here a modern, cosmopolitan city has evolved beneath the snow-capped mountains. The population may be small, but it's clear from the cafés, restaurants and nightclubs that this is a place where people know how to have a good time. However, the scene starts late, and the often eye-watering prices for alcohol and a decent meal force many locals to get their eating and a fair bit of their drinking done at home before they venture out.

Outside the capital, some towns, notably Akureyri in the north, share some of Reykjavík's energy, but most are happy not even to try. The smaller towns are quiet, compact and neat, often no more than a cluster of colourful houses around a church or shop. The pace of life is slow, and the sense of community strong.

Hot Springs and Outdoor Baths

Since the late 1970s the country's only major road, a vast circular route around the coast, has linked village to town, countryside to capital. Most communities are found on or near the ring road, a short distance from the sea, where the land is at its flattest and most fertile. This narrow coastal plain, the only truly habitable part of the country, makes up just one-fifth of Iceland's total area.

Fortunately, much of the most impressive scenery is easily accessible from the ring road. The site of the original Geysir, which gave its name to all geysers around the world, is close to the capital, as is the best outdoor bath on the planet, the Blue Lagoon. The mighty Vatnajökull glacier, at 8,400 sq km (3,200 sq miles) the largest in Europe, reaches down to the sea across the southeast of the country.

To the north, Jökulsárgljúfur National Park (now part of the Vatnajökull National Park) is not only an impressive tongue-twister, even by Icelandic standards, but also home to Europe's largest, most powerful waterfall, Dettifoss, which plummets into the canyon below amid clouds of rainbow-coloured spray. In the north and west, the coastline is splin-

What's in a Name

According to tradition, Iceland owes its name to a Viking adventurer who chanced upon it around AD870. After spending a long hard winter watching his cattle die from the bitter cold and lack of good grazing, he climbed a mountain only to see the fjord choked with drift ice. Wholly disenchanted, he named the place Ísland, literally 'ice land', and promptly departed for the positively balmy climes of his native Norway. Four years later one of his compatriots returned and started the first proper settlement at a place he called Reykjavík, or 'smoky bay', after the plumes of steam he saw rising from nearby thermal springs.

tered by craggy fjords and the sheer granite sides of flat table-top mountains. Further inland, wide valleys rise towards the barren upland plateaux that constitute the interior. This is Europe's last wilderness, a wide expanse of bleak grey lava desert fringed by volcanoes, glaciers and mountaintops, most of it all but inaccessible.

Long Days of Summer

The weather in Iceland can be as varied as the geography. Winters are cold and dark, with a large amount of snowfall. Light relief is provided at night by the spectral glow of the northern lights (*aurora borealis*). It's only in summer, when the temperatures rise and the long days are often bright and sunny, that it's possible to see the full extent of the country properly. Many of the hotels and restaurants, are open only between May and September. Similarly, the bus companies don't run a full service until late June, when the last of the snow has thawed.

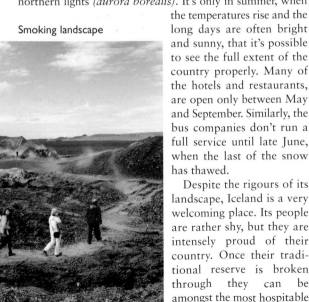

Smoking landscape

Despite the rigours of its landscape, Iceland is a very welcoming place. Its people are rather shy, but they are intensely proud of their country. Once their traditional reserve is broken through they can be amongst the most hospitable people in Europe.

A BRIEF HISTORY

While elsewhere in Europe, civilizations, empires and dynasties came and went, Iceland remained uninhabited and undiscovered. It wasn't until the 8th century AD that Irish monks became the first people known to have set foot on the island, relishing its solitude. They left no physical trace behind either, nor, being all men, any new generation. Within 100 years the peace they had enjoyed was no longer: the Vikings were coming. Much of Iceland's history was chronicled within a few hundred years of the events happening. The *Landnámabók* (Book of Settlements), written in the 12th century, describes in detail the first permanent inhabitants. The sagas, dramatic tales of early Iceland penned 100 years later, give a lot more colour to the story in the form of fiction.

The First Settlers

The country's first settlers were Norwegians escaping political persecution and economic hardship at home. They found Iceland by accident, having already colonised parts of both Scotland and the Faroe Islands. The official 'First Settler' was Ingólfur Arnarson, who enjoyed his first winter so much that in 874 he went to fetch his extended family and friends to come and join him. They brought with them farm animals, paganism and Irish slaves, some of whom would cause mutiny and kill their

Name-drop

Although many Icelanders can trace their families back to the early settlers, family names do not exist. Instead, children absorb their father's first name into their own. A man named Eiríkur Gúðbrandsson might, for example, have a son named Leifur Eiríksson and a daughter named Þórdís Eiríksdóttir.

Viking relics

owners. However, there was no indigenous population for the colonisers to evict or butcher, and the biggest threat they faced was from the elements.

These first Icelanders established farms in the rather more hospitable parts of the country, and within 60 years there were approximately 25,000 people living around the coast. Some basic laws were already in place: a man could claim as much land as he could light bonfires around in one day, so long as each one could be seen from the others. Women could have as much land as a heifer could walk around in a day. Inevitably disputes broke out, which the local chieftains had to resolve. When they failed, there could be bloody battles.

The First Parliament

In AD930 the chieftains got together and agreed on a relatively democratic system of government. A Commonwealth was established, with a national assembly or *Alþingi* meeting for two weeks every summer at Þingvellir. Here, new laws would be agreed and infringements of old laws settled by a system of regional courts. The worst punishment was to be declared an outlaw and banished from the country.

The system wasn't perfect, and there were still some bloody battles – these were, after all, the descendants of

Vikings, who valued courage and honour above all else. Nonetheless this period is now considered to have been a Golden Age, the Saga Age, full of great heroes and wise men.

From Pagans to Christians

Soon, however, things were to change dramatically. Christianity had spread to northern Europe, and the zealous, if bloodthirsty, King Ólafur Tryggvason of Norway wanted Iceland for the new religion too. When his missionaries encountered resistance in the late 10th century he was all for butchering the entire population until the Icelandic chieftain Gizur the White promised to have another go by more peaceful means. Fortunately the lawspeaker, who presided over the Alþingi, was at that time the widely respected Þorgeir. He persuaded both sides to agree to accept his decision in advance and then went off to meditate. He came back and announced that Iceland would become Christian, although pagans could continue to practise their beliefs in private.

Bishoprics, monasteries and schools quickly followed, and books were soon being written for the first time. As a sign of their independence the writers chose to do their work in Icelandic, not Latin. There were so few foreign influences in the centuries to come that the language they used is almost identical to the Icelandic spoken today.

All was not well in the land, however, and Iceland was about to enter its Dark Age. The Hekla volcano outside Reykjavík erupted in 1104, burying nearby farms; over-grazing and soil erosion from excessive tree-felling further reduced the amount of viable land. At the same time the church became greedy and, by imposing tithes, it split the formerly egalitarian society. Some chiefs, who were given church lands or made into senior clergy, found themselves increasingly rich and powerful. Before long the most important families started fighting for supremacy. The Alþingi, which had relied on

Illustration from *Njáls Saga*

people voluntarily accepting its authority, was now powerless to respond.

Civil War and Black Death

Soon the country was in a state of civil war, which was ended only when Norway took sovereignty to help maintain order in 1262. Iceland kept many of its old laws, but 700 years of foreign domination had begun. Revolts and skirmishes continued, while nature also took its toll. Long, harsh winters destroyed farm animals and crops, yet more eruptions covered parts of the country in ash, and the Black Death arrived in Iceland, laying waste to half the population.

Those Icelanders still living were too busy struggling to survive to notice that Denmark had taken over the Norwegian throne and was therefore their new master. But the Danes took little interest in their new acquisition, despite it possessing something the rest of Europe suddenly wanted: cod. Fishing brought new wealth to coastal landowners, but it brought new trouble, too.

English and German adventurers started appearing offshore, fighting among themselves, indulging in piracy and trying to control the trade in dried cod. The English got the upper hand, and this became known as the English Century.

The Danes eventually realised that they were losing out financially. When Denmark tried to ban the English from the country, the latter killed the governor and started bringing in their canons. By 1532, however, the tide had turned, and the English leader was killed in renewed fighting with Germany. However, from then on England let the Danes and the Germans fight among themselves and turned their attentions elsewhere.

The Reformation

The Church was still a dominant force in the early 16th century, and when Scandinavia turned Lutheran during the 1530s it was inevitable that Iceland would soon follow suit. By the middle of the 16th century the transition had taken place, and Protestant Reformation had been well and truly imposed on an unwilling Icelandic population.

The Sagas

Between the 12th and 15th centuries some of the great stories the Icelanders had previously passed on from generation to generation were written down. Collectively known as *The Sagas* (literally 'things told'), they are universally acknowledged as one of the world's most important bodies of medieval literature. Scholars argue about how accurate they are, but for good old-fashioned story telling they are unbeatable. Families are torn apart by feuds, knights ride off to battle in shining armour, saints are saintly, the wicked are truly wicked, and mythical dragons and dwarves stalk the land. They are written in an unemotional style that makes the brutal fates of many of their characters even more shocking. The manuscripts were collected for posterity by Árni Magnússon (1663–1730) and taken off to Copenhagen for safety, but most were then lost in a terrible fire. Árni himself braved the flames to rescue some of them. The surviving *Sagas* weren't returned to Iceland until long after Independence. Perhaps wary of their troubled history, the authorities in Reykjavík keep them under lock and key, although some are occasionally put on display at the Culture House.

National hero

Jón Sigurðsson (1811–69) is a great hero to Icelanders. A scholar and MP, he agitated for independence from Denmark. He helped to achieve limited home rule, but died in 1879, long before sovereignty was restored in 1918.

By this time, Denmark was gaining increased political authority over Iceland, and eventually complete control of the country was passed to Copenhagen. From 1602 all of Iceland's trade had to pass by law through a small group of Danish firms, a move that effectively bankrupted the country. Smallpox then wiped out almost a third of the impoverished population, and, just when it seemed as if matters could not get any worse, thousands more citizens were killed in 1783–4 by massive eruptions that poisoned almost the entire country and caused widespread famine. Denmark considered evacuating the whole surviving population, but decided instead to relax the trading laws a little and give the country a chance to recover.

As it did so, educated Icelanders looked to continental Europe and saw democracy stirring in once-powerful monarchies. Jónas Hallgrímsson, a poet, and Jón Sigurðsson *(see box above)*, a historian, started a fledgling independence movement. By 1843 they succeeded in getting the Alþingi, suspended since 1800, revived as a consultative assembly. A decade later trade was freed up completely. Slowly, prosperity started to return.

In 1874 Denmark, now a constitutional monarchy, returned full legislative powers to the Alþingi. The tithe system was abolished, schooling became compulsory, and the fishing industry was allowed to grow and prosper. By 1900 Iceland had its own political parties. In 1904 it was granted Home Rule and in 1918 gained independence in return for keeping the Danish king as monarch.

War and Peace

Iceland, now trading with England and Germany, was neutral in World War I, although its growing economy was hit by the Great Depression of the 1930s. In World War II control of the North Atlantic was a key strategic objective, and first Britain, then the United States, landed forces in Iceland. Denmark was invaded by Germany, and its ties to Iceland were finally cut when full independence was declared in 1944.

Iceland's strategic location made the new government feel nervous, as the Cold War gripped the western world. In response it joined the UN and then NATO. Still, the decision to allow US forces to return to their wartime bases in 1951 provoked riots in Reykjavík.

When Iceland next went to war, however, it was with a fellow NATO country, Britain. Fortunately nobody was killed, and the so-called Cod Wars, that came and went for

Jón Sigurðsson, leader of the independence movement

30 years after 1952, were no more than a bit of naval muscle flexing. Britain objected to successive extensions to Iceland's territorial waters and sent patrol boats to protect its trawlers. In 1975 it ordered its frigates to ram Icelandic coastguard ships, which had been cutting the cables of British trawlers. Eventually, in 1985, Iceland got its way, and 325km (200-mile) limits became the norm worldwide.

Since the last quarter of the 20th century the country has been increasingly outward looking, attracting foreign businesses and visitors. In 1986 the world's media descended on Reykjavík for a nuclear summit between presidents Reagan and Gorbachev.

Although the European Union's stringent fisheries policy has deterred Iceland from joining that group, all of the carefully considered arguments for and against were rendered void when Iceland's economy disappeared into a black hole in 2008 amidst the worldwide economic crisis. Such a desperate financial situation called for desperate measures, and on 16 July 2009 the new coalition government submitted an application for EU membership, with a view to adopting the euro by 2012.

A young Icelander looks to the future

Although Iceland's economy remains dependent on fishing, the government is keen to diversify, as shown by the controversial hydroelectrically powered aluminium smelting plant in the Eastfjords. All in all, Iceland looks to the future as a proud and independent nation, happy to cooperate with the world community – but reluctant to be dictated to by it.

Historical Landmarks

c.8th century AD Irish monks start to settle on 'Thule'.

c.870 A Norwegian, Hrafna-Flóki, tries to settle in the West Fjords. Foiled by the harsh winter, he calls the land *Ísland* (Iceland).

874 Ingólfur Arnarson and his family and friends settle on Iceland. They name the settlement Reykjavík (Smoky Bay).

930 Creation of the Alþingi parliament.

1000 Christianity is adopted as Iceland's official religion.

13th–14th centuries Norway and Denmark feud over ruling of Iceland.

1389 Huge eruption of Mt Hekla, followed by the Black Death.

15th century England and Germany battle to control trade in cod.

1662–1854 Trade monopoly with Denmark.

1783 Eruption of Laki volcano poisons the land and leads to famine.

1800 Danish King abolishes the Alþingi; it is reinstated in 1843.

1874 Denmark gives the Alþingi autonomy over domestic affairs.

1904 Iceland is granted home rule.

1918 Iceland made a sovereign state (with Danish king as its monarch).

1940 The Alþingi announces it will govern Iceland itself.

1944 Independence from Denmark declared on 17 June.

1949 Iceland becomes a founding member of NATO.

1952–76 Cod Wars (1952, 1958, 1972, 1975) with the UK.

1955 Halldór Laxness wins the Nobel Prize for Literature.

1963 Surtsey island created by an underwater volcanic eruption.

1973 Volcanic eruption on Heimaey island.

1986 Nuclear summit between presidents Reagan and Gorbachev held in Reykjavík .

1994 Iceland enters the European Economic Area.

2000 Mt Hekla eruption in February; earthquakes in June.

2002 Iceland re-admitted to the International Whaling Commission.

2006 Iceland resumes commercial whaling.

2010 The eruption of Eyjafjallajökull spreads a cloud of volcanic ash and brings Europe's air traffic to a standstill.

WHERE TO GO

Iceland is one of the world's most spectacular destinations, with vast empty landscapes illuminated by sparkling, clear sub-arctic air and cosy fishing villages sheltering from Atlantic storms beneath gargantuan cliffs. It's a paradise for anyone with a love of nature and the great outdoors, lent a surreal edge by the presence of the restless tectonic activity beneath and lunar landscape.

Visitors to this country range from the experienced adventure traveller in search of new challenges to those on a two- or three-day stop-over between Europe and North America. Whether you come for several weeks or just a few days there will be no shortage of things to see and do. Iceland's infrastructure is well designed and works efficiently. So whether you prefer to make your own arrangements or join a commercial excursion you'll find everything you need to make your stay a memorable one.

The tourist industry in Iceland works almost exclusively in English, so a lack of Icelandic is not usually a problem. Facilities are constantly improving, and the number of people now visiting Iceland means there is usually a range of options when it comes to choosing tours or means of transport.

REYKJAVÍK

Most visitors start and end their trip in **Reykjavík**, and many are surprised by how small and insubstantial it

North and west

Reykjavík is the world's most northerly capital city, at 64.08°N, and at 21.55°W it is Europe's most westerly capital.

Dynjandi waterfall, the West Fjords

can seem. There is virtually no high-rise building, certainly there are no skyscrapers, and the use of corrugated iron and timber in many of the buildings makes them look almost temporary. In fact, the building materials and layout of the city are very practical and, like everything else in Iceland, are designed with the elements in mind.

Around a third of the country's population live in the capital, where they enjoy fresh air and a magnificent location between the bay and the mountains and glaciers of the interior. Apart from a few major roads around the edge of town, the streets are narrow and sometimes steep. Reykjavík has now earned its stripes as a destination in its own right. Its energetic and distinctive cultural scene is a constant source of fascination, yet it retains a certain slow pace and almost rustic charm that makes it unique amongst the world's capitals. Its manageable size means that almost

Stopping to admire the view at Tjörnin lake

everything you'll want to see is either within walking distance or a short bus or taxi ride away.

Hallgrímskirkja and Vicinity

Hallgrímskirkja spire

The drive into the capital from the airport across the lava fields to the south of the city quickly reveals the central importance of the massive **Hallgrímskirkja** (off Bergþórugata; daily 9am–5pm; free). The church is so enormous that it not only dominates the skyline, it reduces everything else to virtual insignificance. The eye is constantly drawn back to it and its bizarre shape resembling a spacecraft ready for lift-off (curiously, once you return to the city the building becomes much less obtrusive). The church is the most obvious place to begin a visit to Reykjavík, and, unless you are staying nearby, you will almost certainly approach it up the steep Skólavörðustígur. As you head up this street, take time to look in the windows of the art galleries that have sprung up here recently, reflecting how much artistic talent such a small country has produced.

Climb the 73m (240ft) tower – or take the lift – and you are rewarded with the best view of Reykjavík from the viewing platform (daily 9am–5pm; charge). Designed by Guðjón Samúelsson, and in almost constant construction since the end of World War II, it is a monument not only to Christ, but also to Reykjavík's belief that being a small city need not limit its ambitions. The church itself is very bare, as befits its

Reykjavík rooftops

Lutheran status, and there is not much to see except the magnificent **organ**, which is 15m (50ft) high and has more than 5,000 pipes.

Just outside the church is a **statue of Leifur Eiríksson**, Iceland's greatest adventurer, who reached America long before Christopher Columbus. The statue, which is by Alexander Stirling Calder (the father of the more famous A. Calder), was a gift from the US government to mark the Icelandic parliament's 1,000th anniversary in 1930.

Nearby is a museum dedicated to Einar Jónsson (1874–1954), one of Iceland's greatest modern exponents of sculpture and master of symbolism and epic: the **Safn Einars Jónssonar** (Einar Jónsson Museum; Njarðargata; June–mid-Sept Tue–Sun 2–5pm, mid-Sept–May Sat–Sun 2–5pm; charge; www.skulptur.is). The entrance to the museum is on Freyjugata, on the opposite side of the building from the church. Jónsson was virtually a recluse towards the end of his life and many of the 100 or so pieces exhibited here are dark and sombre in character.

Central Shopping Area

Returning to the bottom of Skólavörðustígur brings you to Reykjavík's main shopping street, **Laugavegur**. The name translates literally as 'Hot Spring Road', and it means what it says – it was once the path taken by townspeople who were going to do their washing in the hot pools in Laugardalur *(see page 36)*. Today, thanks to the city's unique geothermal heating system, the same source is used to help to keep the roads ice-free in winter, using underground water piped up from the springs. The street is home to a mixture of international shops, local stores, cafés, bars, restaurants and hotels.

Close to here is the **Þjóðmenningarhúsið** (Culture House, Hverfisgata 15; daily 11am–5pm; charge, Wed free; www. thjodmenning.is). The key exhibit is a fascinating collection of medieval manuscripts containing rare sagas and eddas full of details of life in Iceland and elsewhere in northern Europe from the time of the Vikings onwards. There is also a collection of memorabilia from the struggle for independence. It is all housed in a splendid building, opened in 1909, that was initially intended for the National Library.

Shopping in Laugavegur

The Government District

At the western end of the main shopping street, after it has changed its name to

Bankastræti, is the district devoted to government buildings.

Government House, at the western end of Bankastræti, is not open to the public but is well worth a look from the outside nonetheless. It is one of the oldest houses in the country, dating from 1761 when it was built as a prison. It now houses the offices of the Prime Minister.

On the opposite side of the street there's an imposing **statue of Ingólfur Arnarson**, the first settler, looking out over the Atlantic. Behind him is the National Theatre and to his right are some of the government ministries.

The Icelandic parliament has only 63 members and its headquarters, the **Alþingishúsið** (off Austurvöllur; not open to the public) is almost lost among the surrounding buildings. It is a grey basalt mansion, built in 1881. When parliament is sitting, its debates can be observed from the public gallery (Mon from 3pm, Tue, Wed from 1.30pm, Thur from 10.30pm; free) but they are, of course, in Icelandic.

Alongside the Alþingishúsið is Reykjavík's stone and corrugated iron Lutheran cathedral, the **Dómkirkjan** (Mon–Fri 10am–5pm; free), built in 1785, which has a rather plain facade, but a dramatic interior with arched windows that bathe the place in light.

Reykjavík Welcome Card

Consider investing in a Reykjavík Welcome Card; it can be purchased from tourist offices, bus terminals, museums, the City Hall Information Desk and many hotels for a cost of ISK1,500 for 24 hours, ISK2,000 for 48 hours and ISK2,500 for 72 hours. The card gives access to a great many museums and galleries, the Family Park and Zoo and all of the city's swimming pools. It also entitles the holder to unlimited free travel on the city buses and free internet access at the tourist office.

The square behind the parliament, **Austurvöllur**, has pleasant lawns and is a good place for a picnic. You'll be watched over by one of the great campaigners for independence. The **statue of Jón Sigurðsson**, known as *The Pride of Iceland*, rises above the square. A couple of streets away is another square, **Lækjartorg**, a lively spot with numerous fast-food outlets and coffee bars.

The Dómkirkjan, Reykjavík's Lutheran cathedral

The most tangible signs of Iceland's Viking settlement can be seen at the **Reykjavík 871±2 Settlement Exhibition** (Landnámssýningin, daily 10am–5pm; charge; www.reykjavik 871.is) at Aðalstræti 16. Here you'll find the remains of an oval-shaped Viking-age farmhouse just below the current street level, along with one of the country's most impressive and imaginative exhibitions.

Just to the west, on the banks of **Tjörnin**, a city-centre lake, is **Raðhús** (Reykjavík City Hall, corner of Tjarnargata and Vonarstræti; Mon–Fri 8.30am–7pm, Sat–Sun noon–6pm; free). Opened in 1992, it is an impressive glass and steel construction and is considered an excellent example of modern Nordic architecture. It has a café, an exhibition space and a large relief map of Iceland. The lake itself is home to dozens of ducks and birds.

Alongside the lake is **Listasafn Íslands** (National Gallery of Iceland, Fríkirkjuvegur 7; Tue–Sun 11am–5pm; charge, Wed free; www.listasafn.is). Now renovated, the small gallery has a fine permanent collection of work by Icelandic

Whaling ships, Reykjavík
harbour

artists, including the country's first professional painter Ásgrímur Jónsson (1876–1958), supplemented by changing exhibitions. There is a café on the first floor with internet access. A couple of blocks away is a very different kind of visual experience, the **Volcano Show** (Red Rock Cinema, Hellusund 6a; tel: 845 9548; daily Apr–June, Sept 3pm, 8pm, July–Aug 11am, 3pm and 8pm, Oct–Mar 8pm; charge). The films show 50 years of Icelandic volcanic eruptions all captured on film. Films are in English, French and German at different times of the day and show dramatic pictures of eruptions, including the one in 1964 that created Iceland's newest island, Surtsey.

The Harbour Area

Just north of the government district are the few streets that lead up to the harbour. These are full of cafés, bars and restaurants and are great for just wandering around.

On Tryggvagata is **Hafnarhús** (Harbour House Art Museum; daily 10am–5pm; Thur till 10pm; free; www.listasafn reykjavikur.is), one of three galleries belonging to the Reykjavík Art Museum, situated in the stylishly renovated former warehouse of the Port of Reykjavíc. Here you will find on display a large collection by the internationally renowned Icelandic pop artist, Erró, as well as other contemporary artists from Iceland and elsewhere.

The **harbour** itself is still fully operational, with fishing boats bringing in their catch. Look out for the five black **whaling**

ships, each with a red H on its funnel, tied up together. They have been in the harbour since Iceland banned commercial whaling in 1989 under international pressure. Today's harbour is built on reclaimed land, so you need to go a few streets back to find what used to be the old harbourfront. Here on Hafnarstræti and adjacent Aðalstræti are some of the city's oldest buildings; many of these have been beautifully restored and now house cafés and bars. Café Victor, Hafnarstræti 1–3, for example, was once the **Fálkahúsið**, where the king of Denmark kept his prize falcons. There are two carved wooden falcons on the roof to commemorate the fact. Along the bay to the east is Jón Gunnar Árnason's stunning sculpture *Sólfar SunCraft* (1986), which is based on a classic Viking longboat.

Next to the harbour is the new **Harpa Concert Hall and Conference Centre**, a gleaming glass structure that is set to open in May 2011.

Jón Gunnar Árnason's stainless-steel *Sólfar SunCraft*

Western Reykjavík

You will probably arrive into the west of the city, where the bus terminals and domestic airport are situated, but there is little to tempt you out there again before your departure. The main exception is the refurbished **Þjóðminjasafn Íslands** (National Museum, Hringbraut, Suðurgata 1, junction with Hringbraut; May–mid-Sept daily 10am–5pm, mid-Sept–Apr Tue–Sun 11am–5pm; charge; www.natmus.is), which provides comprehensive insight into the past 1,200 years of Icelandic history. The section on the use of DNA testing is particularly interesting, detailing research work on the teeth of the first settlers in order to determine their origins.

While in the vicinity, have a look too at the **Norræna Húsið** (Nordic House, Sturlugata 5; Tue–Sun noon–5pm; free except for some exhibitions), a Scandinavian cultural centre with a well-stocked library offering free internet access, exhibitions, concerts and a café.

On the other side of the domestic airport, on **Öskjuhlíð** hill is the glass-domed **Perlan** (Pearl), a revolving restaurant that sits on top of six enormous tanks used to store the geothermally heated water that supplies the city. The tanks hold 24 million litres (over 5 million gallons) of hot water and cater for almost half of Reykjavík's water consumption. An impressive man-made geyser has been constructed outside the Perlan, and Öskjuhlíð itself is a pleasantly leafy area thanks to tree-planting schemes and the creation of walking and cycling paths.

Inside the Perlan building, the **Sögusafnið** (Saga Museum; daily, Apr–Sept 10am–6pm, Oct–Mar noon–5pm; charge; www.sagamuseum.is) is a great place to take the children. This is Iceland's equivalent of Madame Tussaud's and an absorbing collection of life-size silicon models of the main characters from the sagas really bring the country's medieval history to life.

The view of the city from Perlan

At the southern edge of Öskjuhlíð is a seawater lagoon, **Nauthólsvík** (free), where the water is heated by the addition of hot water from the hill. The sea water reaches 20°C (68°F), and there's a hot pot that gets even hotter (up to 35°C/95°F). There is a café and a place to hire kayaks, and the Reykjavík Yacht Club is situated alongside.

Eastern Reykjavík

There is more to see on the eastern side of the city. By the sea, isolated on a grassy square, is **Höfði House**. The building is used for government receptions and social functions and hence closed to the public. It was the location for the summit meetings in 1986 between presidents Reagan and Gorbachev to discuss global disarmament. A ghost supposedly haunts the house, but an electrical fault rather than the troublesome spectre was blamed for the fire that damaged the building in 2009.

Reykjavík water babies

Inland is the **Kjarvalsstaðir** ◄Q
(Municipal Gallery, Flókaga-
ta; daily 10am–5pm; charge,
Mon free), another part of
the Reykjavíc Art Museum.
Half the gallery is dedicated
to the huge, colourful, often
abstract landscapes by the
Icelandic artist Jóhannes
Kjarval (1885–1972), while
the other half houses visiting
exhibitions. Further east is
the **Ásmundarsafn** (Ás- ◄R
mundur Sveinsson Sculpture
Museum, Sigtún 105; daily
May–Sept 10am–4pm, Oct–
Apr 1–4pm; charge, Mon free; www.artmuseum.is), a third
part of the Reykjavíc Art Museum. This is modern sculpture
at its best, with huge figures depicting the people of Iceland
as well as mythical characters. The outdoor sculpture garden
is impressive and open at all hours.

S   A short distance to the east is the **Laugardalur** area, a
green belt that has been largely preserved from development.
It serves as the capital's main sports area with a large open-
air, geothermally heated swimming pool, soccer stadium,
sports hall and ice-skating rink. There is also the Viking-
themed mini-rides of the **Family Park** and adjoining **Reykjavík Zoo** (both daily mid-May–Aug 10am–6pm, Sept–
mid-May 10am–5pm; charge; www.mu.is), which contains
domestic farm animals, animals native to Iceland and a small
coldwater aquarium. The nearby **Botanical Gardens** (daily
May–Sept 10am–10pm, Oct–Apr 10am– 3pm; free) have an
impressive collection of 5,000 plants and almost the entire
Icelandic flora.

The Outskirts

Just outside Reykjavík there are a number of sights that can be visited on a short bus or taxi journey. To the east is the **Árbæjarsafn** (Arbær Open-Air Museum; June–Aug daily 10am–5pm; charge; www.arbaejarsafn.is). The original farm was mentioned in the sagas and is now a showcase of how Icelanders used to live. Here, there are old homesteads with turf roofs from all around the country and a church that dates from 1842. The buildings are added to on a regular basis, as the collection expands. There are also exhibitions on the development of public transport and other services in the capital.

To the west is the town of **Hafnarfjörður**, really a suburb of the capital that has developed a major tourist industry of its own. The location is attractive, with parks and cliffs by the sea. **Fjörukráin** (Viking Village, Strandgata 50; www. fjorukrain.is) houses a guesthouse and the nation's only Viking restaurant. The best time to come here is in February when traditional foods such as pickled rams' testicles and

Smoky Bay's Steamy Power

The name Reykjavík, meaning 'smoky bay', was coined by one of the early settlers who mistook the steam rising from the ground for smoke. Inevitably the arrival of man brought pollution in its wake, especially with the burning of fossil fuels. As the city expanded massively in the 20th century, so did the threat from polluted air. The decision, taken in the 1960s, to convert the city to environmentally friendly power sources cut carbon dioxide emissions from the heating system alone from 270,000 tonnes a year to virtually zero. Today, the geothermally heated water that gave the city its name is used to heat its buildings and is even piped beneath the main streets in winter to prevent icing. Reykjavík is arguably the world's greenest capital city.

cured sharkmeat are served up by Viking-clad waiters. It's all very touristy, and by the time you leave you'll never want to see another horned helmet again.

The town also has some fine museums. At Vesturgata 8, the **Hafnarfjörður Museum** (June–Aug daily 11am–5pm, Sept–May Sat–Sun 11am–5pm; charge) is located in the town's former main warehouse and contains an overview of Hafnarfjörður's history. Next door is **Sívertsens-Húsið** (same times), the town's oldest house, which has been restored to its original state, providing an accurate example of an early 19th-century bourgeois home. The **Hafnarborg Arts Centre** (Strandgata 34; Wed–Mon 11am–5pm; charge) is a genuine highlight of the town and has a permanent collection and exhibitions by Icelandic and international artists. There are occasional music recitals and other events.

There is a fine church and **sculpture garden** at Viðistaðir on the northern outskirts of the town.

Viðey and Lundey

Just 1km (⅔ mile) out to sea due north of Reykjavík is the island of **Viðey**, a small but historically significant place full of old buildings, memorials and grottoes. Just up from the jetty is the oldest building in Iceland, Viðeyjarstofa, built in 1755 and now a classy restaurant. The bird life is prolific on Viðey, and there are some impressive basalt columns on the isthmus at the centre of the island. It's small enough to stroll around with ease in an hour or two. Ferries depart from Sundahöfn harbour in Reykjavík between mid-May and August at hourly intervals (for times, tel: 533 5055), and the trip takes less than 10 minutes.

The best chance of seeing puffins close to the capital is on the tiny island of **Lundey**. You can't go ashore, but whale-watching tours depart from Reykjavík harbour between mid-May and mid-August and include a round-the-island trip. Bookings can be made at the harbour in Reykjavík.

THE BLUE LAGOON

One trip out of Reykjavík that should not be missed is to the world's greatest outdoor bath, **Bláa Lonið** (Blue Lagoon, Grindavík; daily mid-May–Aug 9am–9pm, Sept–mid-May 10am–8pm; charge; tel: 420 8800; www.bluelagoon.is). Most hotels will have details of tours, but you can also arrive by public bus. The lagoon is a pool of seawater naturally heated by the geothermal activity below the surface. It sits in the middle of a lava field and you can lounge around

Bathing in the Blue Lagoon

here with warm mud oozing between your toes in wonderfully warm water temperatures of 36–39°C (97–102°F) all year round.

In spite of its evocative name, the lagoon is not a natural phenomenon but a fortuitous by-product of Iceland's geothermal energy usage. The nearby Svartsengi power plant pumps mineral-laden water from up to 2km (1¼ miles) beneath the earth's surface, at a temperature of 240°C (470°F). The superheated water passes through a dual process, on the one hand to generate electricity, and on the other to heat fresh water. This run-off water, rich in silica, salt and other elements, once flowed out into a pool a few hundred metres from the present lagoon's site. Psoriasis and eczema sufferers noticed that bathing in the water seemed to ease their symptoms. Once the word was out, the lagoon was moved to its current location, and state-of-the-art facilities, carefully designed to complement the surrounding landscape, were built around it.

A cave-like sauna is carved into the lava and a thundering waterfall delivers a pounding massage. The complex also contains a spa treatment area, restaurant, snack bar, shop, conference facilities, and, should you care to spend the night, there is a guesthouse just over the lava field. All summer long (June–Aug), however, the changing rooms get crowded and it may be worth getting up early to beat the crowds. If you're impressed by the Blue Lagoon's healing properties, a range of eponymous skin and bathing products are on sale across the island. If you are in the lagoon at the end of the day you can watch the sun set while you soak away life's strains.

Health matters

The Blue Lagoon is officially recognised as a psoriasis clinic by the Icelandic Ministry of Health. Patients come from all over the world to soak up its benefits.

Þingvellir, a national park and site of the original parliament

THE GOLDEN CIRCLE

This 300km (190-mile) round trip from Reykjavík takes in some of the key historical and geological sites in Iceland. They include the original geyser that gave its name to gushing blowholes worldwide, the site of the country's first parliament, and one of its most dramatic waterfalls. You can cover the route on any one of a number of day tours from Reykjavík. They take about seven hours, but include stops at gift shops and eating places along the way. The trip can just about be done by public transport or you could hire a car. The route is well signposted, and parking is good.

Þingvellir

The nearest landmark to the capital on the Golden Circle route is the site of the orginal Alþingi (parliament), established in 930. It is situated in **Þingvellir** (Assembly Plains;

free), a large national park that has enormous political and geographical significance. Unfortunately, there are few actual monuments or buildings to be seen, and you have to use your imagination to picture the events of the past.

There is a well-marked **visitor centre** with maps of the area and large boards outside explaining its significance. Fishing and camping permits can be obtained here. It's worth familiarising yourself with the layout of the park before you set off to explore as it's not that well signposted. The park is situated on top of the line where the North American and

The Parliament at Þingvellir

Þingvellir may feel as if it's in the middle of nowhere, but 1,000 years ago it was the focal point of the country. For two weeks every summer Icelanders flooded into the valley to take part in or just watch the proceedings of the Alþingi (parliament). The position was perfect, with plenty of grazing land for horses, good tracks from the more populated parts of Iceland and a lake teeming with fish to feed the multitudes. Trading and socialising went on continuously while the leaders got on with the serious work of running the country. It was the job of the 36 chieftains from the various regions to agree on new laws, under the supervision of the 'lawspeaker'. A Law Council, made up of four regional courts and a supreme court, dealt with infringements and disputes. Huge fines could be imposed and for the most serious crimes the offenders were outlawed from the country, but the system relied on the population to accept its authority voluntarily. It didn't have the power to stop open warfare from breaking out when disputes couldn't be resolved peacefully. From the mid-16th century the courts gained more power, and public executions took place. Men were beheaded, and women convicted of witchcraft or sexual offences were drowned in the river. Alþingi's last meeting was held here in 1798. After that a national court and parliament was established in Reykjavík.

Eurasian continental plates meet. In fact they are slowly drifting apart at a rate of 2cm (¾in) a year. From the **Almannagjá viewing point** you can see the rift valley clearly as you look towards the lake. The red-roofed church dates from 1859. It stands on the site of a much bigger church that held sway over all the local inhabitants. Below you is the Alþingi site itself. You can walk down into it: a flagpole marks where the leader of the parliament, the law speaker, made his proclamations. Just to the east of the Alþingi the Öxará River flows into a lake, **Þingvallavatn**. There's a 20m (66ft) waterfall, and nearby you can clearly see the layers of ash left by successive eruptions.

Inside Skálholt

Skálholt

Next stop on the Golden Circle is **Skálholt**, about 45km (28 miles) to the east of Þingvellir, and a seat of ecclesiastical, rather than political, power. Skálholt was the site of a bishopric from 1056 until a massive earthquake destroyed its cathedral in the late 18th century. The bishop picked up his cassock and headed for the relative safety of Reykjavík, and it wasn't until 1963 that the present church was finally restored and reconsecrated. It's hard to imagine when you see the church that it was once at the centre of the biggest settlement in Iceland and site of the country's first school. Inside you can see the coffin of one of the early bishops, uncovered during the reconstruction work, and a fine modern mosaic above the altar. Alongside the church there is a

Strokkur in action

conference and cultural centre, where concerts and art exhibitions are staged in summer.

Geysir

Another 20km (12 miles) to the northeast you can see evidence of the one power that both church and state have to respect: nature. There are bigger geysers (*geysir* in Icelandic) in the world, and more impressive ones, too, but this is the site of the original. **Geysir** is one of the few ◄ 6 Icelandic words to have made it into the lexicon of world language. Sadly, the gusher that used to reach heights of 60m (200ft) hasn't performed well for decades. For years Icelanders poured masses of soap powder into the orifice to make it perform, but in the end they gave up. It still erupts a couple of times a day, but generally only to a height of around 10 metres (33ft)

Fortunately, there is the smaller, but more reliable **Strokkur** (literally 'the churn') beside Geysir; Strokkur spurts to a height of around 20m (66ft) every few minutes, without artificial encouragement. Never stand too close to Strokkur – an average of seven tourists are scalded every week during the summer months, mostly from putting their hands in the surrounding water pools to test the temperature.

The whole Geysir area is geothermically active and smells strongly of sulphur (similar to the smell rotten eggs). Walking trails are marked out among the steaming vents and glistening, multicoloured mud formations.

Gullfoss

An example of nature at its most forceful is to be found another 6km (4 miles) along the road to the north. **Gullfoss** 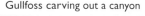 (Golden Falls) is, in fact, two separate waterfalls a short distance apart. Their combined drop is 32m (105ft), and the canyon below is some 2km (just over a mile) long, with basalt columns like the pipes of an organ rising up from the bottom. Trails climb past the waterfall's northern face, allowing you to get within an arm's length of the awesome flow. Wear a raincoat, or the clouds of spray that create dozens of photogenic rainbows on sunny days will douse you from head to foot.

The falls were nearly destroyed by a hydroelectric dam project in the 1920s but the plans were halted, the government instead purchased the falls and made them a national monument.

Gullfoss carving out a canyon

THE WESTMAN ISLANDS

8 ▶ The **Westman Islands**, or *Vestmannaeyjar* to give them their Icelandic name, are a long strip of 16 islands and numerous rocks or skerries about 10km (6 miles) off the south coast of Iceland. Carbon dating has suggested that they may have been the first part of the country to be inhabited. They were created by underwater eruptions, and the process is still on-going: the newest island, Surtsey, emerged from the sea as recently as the mid-1960s. It has been studied with fascination by scientists, not just because of its dramatic appearance, but for the flora and fauna that are taking root and making it their home.

The tourist authorities describe the islands as the 'Capri of the North', although even they wouldn't claim it was anything to do with the weather. The coves and inlets may be reminiscent of the chic Italian island, but the rain and wind

The rugged coastline of the Westman Islands

that batter them for much of the year certainly are not.

Heimaey

The only inhabited island is **Heimaey**, which can be reached by ferry or plane, although low cloud can close the airport at short notice. It has a pretty little town, but most visitors come for the surrounding countryside and **bird cliffs**. Hundreds of

Heimaey

thousands of puffins come here every year to nest and breed on the precipitous cliffs. You can reach them on foot or take a boat out and get a better view from the sea. You might also see whales and seals in the waters around the islands. (Keikó, the killer whale that starred in the Hollywood film *Free Willy* lived in the harbour here for a few years after a public campaign in the US to have him returned to the wild. He died in December 2003 in Norway.)

The other big draw of Heimaey is the landscape. Two dramatic cones rise up just outside the town: the volcano, Helgafell, and a much newer mountain, Eldfell, created in a massive eruption in 1973 that almost buried the town. In the early hours of 23 January 1973 a fissure nearly 2km (1-mile) long opened up on the eastern side of Helgafell. Red hot lava started to spurt into the sky heralding an eruption that was to last for the next six months. The threat to the town was immediate and the entire 5,000-strong population was taken off to the mainland. Flying bombs of molten lava crashed through windows or melted through roofs, and a colossal river of lava made its way towards the town. Many houses collapsed under the weight of falling ash and by the time the flow stopped a third of Heimaey had been destroyed. The harbour was saved at the last minute and to this day nobody is sure whether this was just luck or whether the millions of tons of seawater that the emergency services poured onto the advancing river of rock did the trick. Either way the harbour had a new wall and much better protection from the elements. When it was all over the island was 2.2 sq km (½ sq mile) larger, and the new mountain of Eldfell had been created. At the edge of the lava, the rather curious Pompei of the North project has excavated the ruins of one house, formerly Suðurvegur 25, and aims to dig out another seven as a reminder of the destruction.

Around the island there are numerous walks, the best of which is off to the west coast and the valley of Herjólfsdalur. Venture a little further and you will reach some of the best bird cliffs, where you can get remarkably close to the puffins.

The Westman Islanders are great sports enthusiasts. There are four football fields on the islands and a modern sports centre with a pool. You can easily take in some fishing, rock climbing or golf if you stay for long enough.

The Puffin Population

The puffin is a national symbol in Iceland as well as a national dish. It is a member of the auk family and has a multicoloured beak and bright orange legs and feet. Puffins are highly sociable, often standing about in groups and nesting in large colonies. They fish together, too, forming wide rafts out to sea. They can dive to 60m (200ft) in search of fish, but also eat plankton in winter. They rarely travel far from their colony while raising their young. Both parents incubate a single egg. The males and females look very similar, but neither grow much more than 30cm (12in) in height. They produce a dark meat, like duck but less fatty, which is often served with a blueberry sauce.

The puffin is Iceland's national symbol

THE SOUTH COAST

The stretch of highway that runs east along the south of Iceland is a mixture of long, almost featureless lava fields and wonderful views of the mountain and glaciers that come down to the sea in the southeast. It has a reputation as the wettest part of the country, but if the weather holds it is also one of the most dramatic.

As you leave Reykjavik and pass **Selfoss**, heading east, look out for **Mt Hekla**. On a fine day its cone provides a perfect backdrop to Reykjavík, but it's frequently shrouded in cloud. It's an active volcano that has wiped out farming in the surrounding area several times and erupted every 10 years or so since 1970; however, it can still be climbed fairly easily. Discover route details and background history at **Heklumiðstöðin** (Hekla Museum, Brúarlundi, Landsveit, tel: 487 6587; June–Aug daily 10am–6pm; charge).

Þórsmörk

You are now entering saga country and, in particular, the setting for the most bloody of the sagas – that which tells the story of the wise and decent Njál and the gruesome end that met most of his friends and family. Much of the action took place at the Alþingi at Þingvellir *(see page 42)*, but there was more than a little blood-letting near the village of Hvolsvöllur where there is now an Icelandic Saga Centre with background information on the various tales. Here, there is a turning northeast to **Þórsmörk**, a beautiful valley that is well worth the detour. City dwellers from Reykjavík flock here at weekends to enjoy the wooded walks and lovely views.

East of Þórsmörk is **Skógar**, home to a meticulously managed folk museum (June–Aug daily 9am–6pm, May and Sept 10am–5pm, Oct–Apr Mon–Fri 11am–4pm; charge; www.skogasafn.is) housing a 6,000-piece collection.

There is a summer Edda Hotel at Skógar, as well as the splendid waterfall, Skógafoss, the sheer fall of which offers one of south Iceland's best photo opportunities. The trek from here to Þórsmörk, passing between the ice-caps of Eyjafjallajökull (the glacier's underlying volcano erupted in 2010, throwing up a black ash plume into the atmosphere and closing down European air space for several days) and Myrdalsjökull over the Fimmvörðuháls pass, is popular with the hardy and becomes quite crowded, particularly in July. There are two huts between the ice-caps: one is an emergency shelter; the other is pre-bookable.

Skógar homestead

The beautiful valley of Þórsmörk

Vík

Continuing east, the next major stop is the coastal town of **Vík**, or, to give it its full name, Vík í Mýrdal (Bay of the Marshy Valley). It's a pretty little town whose symbol of a smiling yellow face greets you everywhere, possibly to try to counter its reputation as the rainiest place in Iceland. Most people come here for the black volcanic sand, cliffs and birdlife. Three steeples of stone, known as **Reynisdrangar** (Troll Rocks), rise out of the sea. Legend has it they are the figures of trolls that turned to stone when they failed to get under cover before the sun hit them. Whatever their origin, they are inhabited by colonies of Arctic tern in the summer.

The road crosses more barren fields of lava and *sandur*, a mix of silt, sand and gravel. Oddly shaped boulders are partly overgrown with lichens, helping to give the area a somewhat other-worldly feel. Little wooden bridges cross the rivers, reducing the highway to one lane. In the middle of all

11

Rock formations near
Kirkjubæjarklaustur

this is the tiny hamlet of **Kirkjubæjarklaustur**, a good place to pick up provisions. While doing so, you can reflect on the power of prayer, for it was here that the local pastor delivered his 'Fire Sermon', which believers will tell you halted the flow of lava during the Lakagígar eruption of 1783 and saved the church. A memorial chapel, built in 1974, commemorates the miracle.

A rough road, which is accessible only to four-wheel-drive vehicles, goes from Kirkjubæjarklaustur to the **Lakagígar Crater Row**, where you can see some of the effects of the 1783 eruptions that lasted for 10 months and were known as the Skaftáreldar (Skaftá river fires). The eruption was the largest recorded in the world, and the lava produced was equivalent to 12 cubic km (7½ cubic miles). Most of Iceland's livestock died from the poisonous fumes. Some 100 craters extend for 25km (15 miles) up to the glacier; the surrounding lava field is dotted with caves and other lava formations. It takes several hours to see them properly, but there are amazing views from the top of Laki itself – a climb of about an hour.

Vatnajökull

12 ▶ The massive **Vatnajökull**, the biggest ice-cap in Europe, is almost 150km (90 miles) across and dominates the southeastern corner of Iceland. Driving around the ring road you can get fascinating glimpses of it as it breaks through the

mountains. To get close to the ice-cap, though, you have to leave the main road and head inland. Its size and beauty, however, is best appreciated from the air, particularly on an internal flight from Reykjavík to Egilsstaðir or Höfn.

In October 1996 Vatnajökull was besieged by the world's media when a fissure 4km (2½ miles) long opened beneath the surface of the glacier. Within two days a 10km (6-mile) column of steam was rising above the ice.

Massive flooding was predicted, but the eruption fizzled out, and the journalists departed. Then, on 5 November, the ice dam broke and a huge surge of water burst forth, destroying bridges and roads and carrying massive ice blocks with it.

A number of smaller valley glaciers, all linked to Vatnajökull, are most clearly visible from the road. One of these, Skaftafellsjökull, stops close to the **Skaftafell National Park** ◄ **13**

The glacier lagoon at Jökulsárlón

(visitor centre: May–Sept daily 8am–6pm). In the shadow of Iceland's highest peak, **Hvannadalshnúkur** (2,120m/ 6,950ft), this is serious walking territory and very popular in summer. But with so many trails into the hills, it's not difficult to find solitude.

Hikers take day-long round trips to the higher moorlands and peaks, such as those at **Kristínartindur**. Among the shorter walks is the route up to **Svartifoss** (Black Falls), named after the surrounding sombre cliffs of basalt.

In 2008, Europe's largest national park, **Vatnajökull**, was created, by joining together the Jökulsárgljúfur and Skaftafell national parks with a large protected area.

Svartifoss, the Black Falls

Jökulsárlón

Continuing east, the next major point of interest is the extra-ordinary glacier river lagoon at **Jökulsárlón**. This photogenic spot **14** is just off the road where a small bridge crosses the mouth of the lake. Here great slabs of ice, some as big as houses, that have broken off the **Breiðamerkurjökull** valley glacier float eerily in the water. Boat crui-ses operate around Jökulsárlón several times daily in summer, weav-ing among the glistening ice forma-tions; your guide may even pull a 1,000-year old piece of ice out of the water for you to admire.

Höfn

The final outpost in southeastern Iceland is the town of **Höfn**, which translates simply as 'har- **15** bour'. If you are heading for the Eastfjords *(see page 76)* by public transport you might find yourself having to stay overnight here. It's not the most exciting of places, unless you fancy examining the fish- freezing plant. However, if the skies are clear, there are good views back over the glacier. Tours of the glacier by four-wheel drive can be organised, but if your budget doesn't stretch to that, visit the Glacier Exhibition in the same building as the tourist office (Haf-narbraut 30; June–Aug daily 10am–6pm, May and Sept 1–6pm, Oct–Apr 1–4pm; charge) telling you all you need to know about glaciers.

Hvítserkur, a basalt stack flecked with guano

THE NORTH COAST

If you are restricted to one part of the country in addition to Reykjavík, there is a good chance you will choose the north coast. It's the most accessible region to reach and, in many ways, the liveliest. Akureyri is generally considered to be the capital of the north, and Húsavík is the best point of departure outside Reykjavík for whale-watching. Despite being close to the Arctic Circle, the north also has the best weather, and temperatures can reach 20°C (68°F) or more in summer. The coastline is very dramatic in places, and there are some huge fjords – a feature that is almost completely lacking in the south.

Akureyri

Whether you fly, drive or take a bus you are almost certain to end up in **Akureyri**. It's an attractive place and has a lot more life about it than most provincial towns. It is home to the only professional theatre in Iceland outside the capital, as well as the only university. Many parts of the country suffer from an exodus of young people, but not Akureyri, which has a youthful feel about it. In summer the town is busy with tourists; in winter it's a major destination for conferences.

Akureyri is surrounded by high mountains, which are up to 1,500m (5,000ft) tall and snowcapped for much of the year. Green and lush in comparison to many other towns, it even has its own forest and a golf course (every June the Arctic Open tees off under the midnight sun). Akureyri is also a good starting point for visiting some of the most beautiful parts of the country, both to the east and the west.

The centre of town is compact. The main shopping street is the pedestrianised **Hafnarstræti**. This is where the hustle and bustle (such as it is) of this small town's life takes place. An Akureyri institution, the Bautinn restaurant (tel: 462 1818) at no.92 sits on a crossroads and is a good place to watch the world go by. Hafnarstræti runs from close to the huge main church *(see below)* towards the rather nondescript town square, Ráðhústorg. Running east from the square is Strandgata, which has become the trendy corner of town; this leads down to the port, where cruise liners dock in summer.

The church steeples of the **Akureyrarkirkja** (daily 10am–noon, 1–5pm; free) tower over the town and are most dramatic at night when spotlit against the dark sky. The church was designed by the architect Guðjón

Akureyrarkirkja

Samúelsson, who was also responsible for the vast Halls-grímskirkja in Reykjavík *(see page 27)*. Inside is a fine stained-glass window from the original cathedral at Coventry in the English Midlands. The window was removed at the start of World War II before the cathedral was destroyed by bombs; it was rescued from a London antiques shop and now forms the centrepiece of an impressive display that also features scenes from Iceland's own history.

Having clambered up to the church there is a gentler climb to another of the town's main attractions, the **Lysti-garðurinn** (Botanical Gardens; Eyrarlandsvegur; June–Sept Mon–Fri 8am–10pm, Sat–Sun 9am–10pm; free). The gardens are famed for its 7,000 species of local and foreign flowers blooming outside in Akureyri's warm microclimate. The gardens were set up by a local women's association in 1912 to provide a relaxing atmosphere for families. There are species from southern Europe, Africa, South America and Australasia, as well as examples of just about every variety that grows in Iceland. The gardens are very well kept, and are the perfect place to relax on a sunny day.

Akureyri was the childhood home of the Jesuit priest, Jón Sveinsson, author of the Nonni series of children's books. At Aðalstræti 54 you can visit the restored wooden house he once lived in, **Nonnahús** (June–Aug daily 10am–5pm; charge). His books have been translated into 40 languages.

Fishing in Akureyri

The **Minjasafnið á Akureyri** (Akureyri Municipal Museum; Aðalstræti 58; June–mid-Sept daily 10am–

The Botanical Gardens

5pm, mid-Sept–May Sat only 2–4pm; charge) has a wide collection of everyday items that date as far back as the settlement in the 9th century, including a beautifully painted pulpit. The church here is still used for weddings. **Listasafn Akureyrar** (Kaupvangsstræti 24; Tue–Sun noon–6pm; charge) is the town's Art Gallery and offers visitors one of the best insights into the town's present-day cultural life.

The town's **swimming pool** (Þingvallastræti 2; tel: 461 4460; charge) is one of the best in the country, with facilities including a waterslide, hot tubs, a steam room and sauna. Attached is a family park with mini-golf, electric cars and other distractions for children.

An hour's walk south of the town is one of Iceland's few wooded areas at **Kjarnaskógur**. Given the shortage of trees in Iceland this is considered something of an attraction, and the townspeople flock here on sunny weekends. There is a children's play area, picnic sites and a jogging track.

Big In Iceland

Iceland's tallest man, Jóhann Kristinn Pétursson, known as Jóhann the Giant, was an impressive 2.34m (7ft 7in) tall. Born in 1913, he worked in circuses and shows across Europe and the United States. He returned to Dalvík late in his life and died there in 1984.

Eyjafjörður

From Akureyri two roads fork off to the north along each side of Eyjafjörður fjord. The cluster of towns and villages on the banks of the fjord are hemmed in close to the water by high mountains. The land here is particularly fertile, and the mild climate makes it good farming territory. It's a suitable area for exploring both on land and at sea, with ferry links to the islands of Grímsey and Hrísey.

Dalvík, a fishing village about an hour's drive north of Akureyri, is the main centre on this side of the fjord. The town was rebuilt after an earthquake in 1934 demolished half the buildings, but the harbourfront is still attractive. The town has a good outdoor swimming pool and an interesting museum, **Byggðasafnið Hvoll** (Karlsbraut; June–Aug daily 11am–6pm, Sept–May Sat 2–5pm; charge), in the house of Iceland's tallest man, Jóhann Kristinn Pétursson (*see box above*). It contains photographs of him and many of his possessions as well as examples of local wildlife.

From Dalvík you can catch a ferry to the island of **Grímsey**. The Arctic Circle runs through the centre of this island, and you can get a certificate for crossing it. The small settlement of **Sandvík** has some basic services, including a swimming pool. The community centre commemorates the island's benefactor, Daniel Willard Fiske, a 19th-century American chess champion who had read about its reputation for producing great chess players since Viking days. He left money for a school and library to be built and donated

11 marble chess boards. The locals still celebrate his birthday on 11 November although, a little ungratefully, hardly any of them play chess any more.

Most visitors come to Grímsey for the extensive **birdlife** – the craggy cliffs on the north and east of the island are home to about 60 species, including puffins, kittiwakes and razorbills. You can explore on your own or find a local guide in the town. The only proper road runs along the west side of Grímsey from Sandvík to the airport, from where there are regular flights to Akureyri. The runway has to be regularly cleared of birds, and this is sometimes done by incoming flights buzzing the airstrip before coming round again to land.

From Árskógssandur, just south of Dalvík, a ferry departs every hour for the 15-minute trip out to the island of **Hrísey**, another choice destination for bird lovers. In particular, the island is a haven for the fearless ptarmigan; they are prolific all year round, although their number swells in the autumn, and they can often be seen waddling down the streets. There are almost 40 species of birds on the island, and it is an important breeding ground for eider ducks and Arctic tern.

On the eastern side of the fjord the first place of interest is the fishing village of **Svalbarðseyri**. According to local folklore, this is home to a large community of elves who live in the cliffs behind the village. Even if this sounds all rather unlikely, you are still sure to be enchanted here by the rugged coastline.

At **Laufás**, around 30km (19 miles) north of Akureyri, there is a magnificent exam-

Golden plover

Sacred art at Hólar í
Hjaltadal cathedral

ple of a 19th-century turf farmhouse, maintained by the Icelandic National Museum (daily mid-May–mid-Sept 9am–6pm; charge). Inside there is a multitude of effects showing how life was lived here more than 100 years ago. The timber church dates from 1865.

West of Akureyri

On the route west, the tiny village of **Hófsós** is home to **Vesturfarasetrið** (Icelandic Emigration Centre; daily June–Aug 11am–6pm; charge). If you think you are of Icelandic descent, this is the place to come to try and trace your roots. There is a good exhibition telling the story of those Icelanders who emigrated west to the New World. Next door is a well-preserved traditional warehouse made from Danish imported timber in 1777.

Hólar í Hjaltadal, 25km (15 miles) southeast and inland from the coast road, was once a thriving cultural and religious centre. Until the Reformation it was a great seat of learning, with monks studying the scriptures and transcribing manuscripts. It housed the country's first printing press, dating from 1530. A red-stone **cathedral** (ask at the neighbouring college for entry), dating from 1759–63, commemorates its religious past. There is sacred art and sculpture on display as well as a modern mosaic by the artist Erró. The bones of the last Catholic bishop in Iceland, Jón Arason, are buried here. He was beheaded in 1550 for resisting the spread of the protestant Reformation.

Among the most important historical sites in Iceland is  **Þingeyrar**, 85km (53 miles) further west. It was the home of one of the first regional assemblies as well as the first monastery in 1133. It was here that many of the sagas were written, and other texts were transcribed by the monks. The monastery disappeared after the Reformation, but there is an impressive 19th-century church, **Þingeyrarkirkja**, made of basalt, that is visible for miles around. The interior has a dramatic blue ceiling with 1,000 gold stars painted on it, white walls and green pews. The altarpiece, which was made in Nottingham, England, came from the old monastery.

Húsavík

To the northeast of Akureyri, **Húsavík** occupies a beautiful setting, nestled among high cliffs and facing out over the Arctic. Not surprisingly the sea has always been a dominant fac-

Exterior of Hólar cathedral

On the look-out for whales

tor in the town's development, and today people flock here for **whale-watching tours**, for which Húsavík is renowned.

Down at the harbour is the **Húsavík Whale Museum** (open daily June–Aug 9am–7pm, May and Sept 10am–5pm; charge; www.whalemuseum.is), Iceland's only museum dedicated to these captivating mammals. It contains photographs, models and skeletons to help explain the life-cycle, habits and biology of whales. If you are interested in some of the sea's smaller inhabitants, and how they find their way on to our dinner plates, the centre will also organise visits to the nearby fish processing factory. Húsavík also has an excellent natural history museum, **Safnahúsið**, (Stórigarður 17; June–Aug daily 10am–6pm, Sept–May Mon–Fri 9am–4pm, Sun 4–6pm; charge) in the same building as the town library. As well as memorabilia from old houses and farms, there is a reconstruction of a Viking longboat, various old weapons, exhibits of flora and fauna and, the item of which they are most proud, a stuffed polar bear captured on the island of Grímsey in 1969. The maritime section contains a broad range of exhibits reflecting the town's historical dependence on the sea. The library offers internet access.

Flushed with success in its former home in Reykjavík, the **Íslenzka Reðasafn** (Icelandic Phallological Museum; late-May–early-Sept daily noon–6pm; charge) has now moved to Heðinbrant 3a in Húsavík. On display are more than 150 penises from every mammal found in Iceland or in its wa-

Whales and Whaling

For many visitors, Iceland's attitude to whaling is perplexing. In almost every other way the country has a magnificent record for environmental protection and respect for nature. But whaling is a topic that arouses passionate feelings in Iceland today – a 2009 Gallup poll found that 77.4 percent of Icelanders support the commercial hunt.

The abundance of whales off Iceland's coasts led inevitably to them being caught and killed for food. In 1948 this developed into a commercial whaling industry that continued until 1989.

In March 1999 the Icelandic parliament voted by a large majority to resume commercial whaling. Three years later Iceland was finally re-admitted to the International Whaling Commission, despite the Icelandic government's continued objections to the worldwide moratorium on whaling (albeit for scientific purposes), which caused an outcry when announced in summer 2003.

To many outside observers, the 2006 decision to resume commercial hunting might have appeared self-defeating. Tourist leaders were quick to point out that butchering whales for the domestic food market was totally at odds with the nascent whale-watching industry. However, tourist numbers have continued to rise since 2006. The new coalition government issued a press release in 2009, stating their belief that whale-watching and whale-hunting can exist side by side.

ters, including whales, horses, foxes and a polar bear that drifted into one of the fjords on an iceberg. However, it's just a matter of time before a human penis joins the collection: four donors have bequeathed their members to the museum.

The **church** (Garðarsbraut; daily June–Aug 9am–noon, 1–5pm; free), an impressive wooden building in the shape of a cross, was built in 1906–7 to seat 450 people. The altarpiece features several of the town's residents who posed for a depiction of the resurrection of Lazarus.

There is a well-kept park alongside the river, with a duck-pond attracting long-tailed squaws and eiders. On the southern edge of the town there is a nine-hole golf course, while further south are two man-made warm lagoons, one with free trout fishing. Boat trips from the harbour go out to two small islands: **Lundey** (Puffin Island) and **Flatey** (Flat Island). Don't be confused, there's another Lundey near Reykjavík, and another, much more interesting Flatey off the west coast *(see page 83)*.

East of Húsavík, **Þórshöfn** is another place that dates back to the saga times. It grew considerably in the early 20th century during the peak of the herring boom and is still predominantly a fishing town.

Húsavík harbour

Britain's Prince Charles used to favour **Vopnafjörður**, 60km (37 miles) to the southeast, for fishing holidays. He must have arrived by air, as the roads around here are among the worst in Iceland. The locals will tell you that Santa Claus lives on the nearby **Smjörfjöll** – at least he is able to travel freely by sleigh.

The falls at Goðafoss

LAKES, VOLCANOES, CANYONS AND FALLS

Within easy striking distance of both Akureyri and Húsavík are some of the most impressive geological formations in Iceland. These include two massive waterfalls, Dettifoss and Goðafoss, and Jökulsárgljúfur National Park *(see page 73)* which encloses a spectacular canyon with falls of its own. Lake Mývatn, home to a huge variety of ducks, is surrounded by active geothermal areas, craters and bizarre rock formations. A good road circles the lake close to the shore.

The perfectly proportioned falls at **Goðafoss** are easily reached on the drive into the area from the north. The 'Waterfall of the Gods' was so-named because it was here in the year 1000 that the law-speaker Þorgeir decided Iceland should convert to Christianity before throwing his pagan carvings into the waters.

Lake Mývatn

Although small, **Reyk-jahlíð**, at the northeast corner of Lake Mývatn, is nonetheless the best place to base yourself, and tours of the surrounding area can easily be organised from here. The main sight in the village is its **church**, which is surrounded by hardened lava. A major eruption in 1729 brought lava streaming down from the hills. While it obliterated nearby farmland, it miraculously skirted around the church. Tradition says it was the power of prayer that protected it, although the walls around the cemetery may have helped.

Lake Mývatn

Despite its name, **Lake Mývatn** (Midge Lake) is one of the highlights of a visit to Iceland. Midges and flies love the shallow water at the lake's edge, but they rarely bite, and you can get a hat with netting attached to keep them out of eyes, ears and mouth. The lake, and the **Laxá River** that flows out from the west, are renowned for the variety of **birds** they attract. The area is protected by law, and there are wardens to help visitors enjoy themselves without harming the ecology.

With the peaks of the Krafla volcano and Mt Hverfjall as a backdrop, Lake Mývatn has a serenity that belies the churning geothermal activity just below the surface of the surrounding land. The land around the shore is generally flat, with just a few small hills and mini craters, making it ideal territory for gentle hiking. The Nature Conservation Agency publishes a list of suggested trails. It's worth carrying binoc-

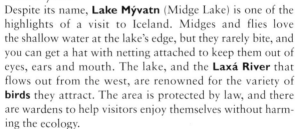

ulars because, whether you are an avid birdwatcher or not, the number and variety of ducks and other birdlife here is extraordinary *(see box below)*.

At the southern end of the lake, **Skútustaðir** has a hotel, church and café-restaurant and facilities for horseriding and hiring bikes. Close to the shore there is a collection of **pseudocraters**, which look like mini volcanoes. In fact they were created when molten lava ran over the marshland. The water below came to the boil and burst through the lava sheet to form cones. Most of the islands in the middle of the lake were formed in the same way.

The Ducks and Birds of Mývatn

According to Iceland's Nature Conservation Agency, more species of ducks are believed to inhabit Lake Mývatn and the Laxá River than anywhere else in the world. Along with geese, swans and other birds, there are tens of thousands of these birds, all attracted by the shallow water, plentiful food and space for nesting.

The most common varieties are the tufted duck, scaup, wigeon, teal and red-breasted merganser. Harlequin ducks live on the rivers in large numbers, and the common scooter, a diving breed, is widely seen on the west side of the lake. Some rare breeds bring ornithologists to Lake Mývatn from all over the world. The barrow's goldeneye is only found here and in North America, for example. In the Rockies, where the species originates, these birds lay their eggs in holes in tree trunks; here, they lay them in holes in the lava. The Slavonian grebe builds floating nests close to the shore. The gadwall and red-necked phalarope are common all over the lake.

Other breeds you are likely to see include whooper swans, greylag geese, Arctic tern and the black-headed gull. Ptarmigans are common, and there are several pairs of gyrfalcon nesting here, along with smaller numbers of short-eared owl and merlin.

The Laxá River contains salmon, brown trout and Arctic char, but you'll need to buy a licence if you want to fish. Further north is the peak of **Vindbelgjarfjall** (530m/1,735ft), which can be climbed by a fairly steep path at the back of the mountain for some fantastic views. From here, the road passes through wetlands containing some of the biggest concentrations of birdlife, before returning to Reykjahlíð.

Geothermal Sites

There is plenty of evidence to indicate just how close the geothermal activity is to the surface in this part of Iceland – you may well see gases rising from fissures in the lava around Reykjahlíð. The local swimming pool here is naturally heated, and there are numerous ovens for baking bread in the hot earth or for smoking fish using dried sheep dung. You can try both at the local restaurants.

On the southern edge of town the hot springs at **Storagjá** can be reached via a ladder and rope. They have cooled in recent years and become infested with algae, which dissuades most potential swimmers. Another pool, **Grótagjá**, on the Egilsstaðir road, suffers from the opposite problem – it's too hot for most people, but is well worth a look as it's inside a naturally formed cavern in the lava. A popular tourist attraction, the Cowshed Café (Vogafjós; May–Sept daily 7.30am–11pm) backs onto a milking shed, so you can watch the working life of the farm while you sample Icelandic ice-cream. Continuing in the same direction, the newly opened **Jarðböðin** nature baths

> ### Daily bread
>
> The local tradition of underground baking involves mixing rye dough with yeast and molasses, pouring the mixture into old milk cartons and baking them in holes covered by metal sheets for a day. The result is a heavy but moist steam bread known as *hverabrauð*.

The Grótagjá pool

(daily June–Aug 9am–midnight, Sept–May noon–10pm; charge), are the north's answer to the Blue Lagoon, though without the crowds. Supplied with geothermally heated water at 38–40°C (100–104°F) from the nearby Bjarnarflag borehole, the pool here covers 5,000 sq m (5,980 sq yds) and contains a mix of minerals, silicates and micro-organisms. It is the perfect place to sit and soak for an hour or two.

A road off to the north takes you up towards the **Krafla volcano**. There have been eruptions in and around Krafla for much of the past 3,000 years. The so-called Krafla Fires of 1977–84 left a huge field of lava that is still steaming today. The eruption threatened the **Leirbotn power station**, but stopped just short and you can visit the plant for free most afternoons. Further up the road is a perfectly rounded crater **Viti** ('Hell'), which was formed in 1724 and has since flooded. Its huge size, the strange blue tint to the water and the sheer drop down from the rim makes it an awesome

Ásbyrgi canyon

sight. From the Krafla car park you can visit a second crater, **Sjálfskapar Viti**, or 'Home-made Hell', so-called because it was formed when a borehole being drilled for the power station exploded. Fortunately, nobody was killed, but debris from the rig was found for miles around. A well-marked track leads up to the **Leirhnjúkur crater** and the **Krafla Caldera**, formed in the mid-18th century and now a colourful collection of bubbling mud-holes encrusted with sulphur. You can walk around them, but stick to the well-worn paths. Note that the lighter coloured soil is thin and could give way under a person's weight.

Close to the eastern edge of Lake Mývatn is the enchanting **Dimmuborgir basin**, a vast, 2,000-year-old field of contorted volcanic pillars, some extending as high as 20 metres (65ft). There is a helpful visitor centre and café (June–Aug daily 9am–10pm, reduced hours Apr, May and Sept) here, offering guided walks in the area. A viewing platform looks out over the expanse, and visitors can wander about among the haunting arches, caves and natural tunnels. The most famous formation is Kirkjan (the Church), a cave that looks like the interior of a Gothic cathedral, and a 3-metre (16ft) hole that provides an amusing photo opportunity. You have to keep to the paths to protect the rock from damage, but it's a lovely spot to explore.

Jökulsárgljúfur National Park

North of Mývatn, **Jökulsárgljúfur National Park** straddles part of Iceland's second-longest river, the **Jökulsá á Fjöllum**. More than half the country's plant species are to be found here, but most visitors are drawn by the geology of the area.

Jökulsárgljúfur itself is a vast canyon up to 120m (395ft) deep and 500m (1,640ft) wide, and its name means 'glacier river canyon'. There are numerous waterfalls along its route. The two most impressive of them, **Dettifoss** (Europe's most powerful falls) and **Selfoss**, are situated at the southern boundary of the park. At the northern tip is the information office where you can acquire details of the area's many walking trails and sights.

◀ 23

From the tourist office a road leads down towards the great horse-shoe shaped **Ásbyrgi canyon**, a 90m (295ft) semicircle of rock flecked with colourful lichens. The first Viking settlers believed the canyon was formed by Sleipnir, the god Odin's flying horse, crashing a giant hoof into the earth. There are three campsites in the park if you want to stay and explore the area.

Tern attack

The Arctic tern is nature's own divebomber. If disturbed, it flies down from a great height and attacks while squawking furiously. The best way to ward off the terns is to walk around with a clenched fist or newspaper held up above your head.

Seyðisfjörður is surrounded by mountains

EASTERN ICELAND

The eastern part of Iceland is one of the least-visited areas of the country and, as a result, has a less well-developed tourist industry. There is not as much volcanic activity here but overall the region has a quiet, gentle feel, making it pleasant to visit. The East enjoys some of the sunniest weather in the country– and the undulating farmland and rugged coast are ideal for walking.

For the past decade, the region has been at the centre of the greatest environmental debate Iceland has ever known when it was chosen as the site for an immense dam and aluminium smelter. Construction on the smelter began in Reyðarfjörður 'n 2004, and was completed by 2008. It transformed the local ~onomy and created scores of new jobs, yet its power is sup- ~d by the Kárahnjúkar Dam, which was built in an envi- ~entally sensitive part of the interior.

Egilsstaðir

With its airport and its pivotal position on the ring road, **Egilsstaðir** is the most-visited town in the region. It's not the loveliest of places, but it's a good base for trips to the lakes and mountains to the south of it. There is a modern concrete **church**, designed to reflect the surrounding mountains, and the excellent **Minjasafn Austurlands** (East Iceland Heritage Museum, Tjarnabraut; June–Aug, Tues–Sun, 11am–5pm; charge). It's packed with all manner of crafts and folklore exhibits and has an indoor turf farmhouse, no bigger than a large shed, that was inhabited until 1964. Also on show are three stone crosses excavated near Seyðisfjörður, thought to date from the mid-12th century. At the northern end of the town is a good-sized **swimming pool**, which is ideal for relaxing in after a day's walking.

Lögurinn and Snæfell

The lake of **Lögurinn** runs 30km (19 miles) south from Egilsstaðir, carrying the **Largarfljót River** from the Vatnajökull ice cap to the sea. The road around it is rough in places, but, unusually for Iceland, the banks are forested, especially over on the eastern side. The lake is in a deep glacial valley and is said to be home to the **Lagarfljótsormur monster**, a creature not unlike Scotland's Loch Ness monster, although nobody seems to have got close enough to be sure.

The forest at **Hallormsstaður** is the showcase for Iceland's efforts at re-forestation after the indiscriminate

Snake charm

According to folklore, a young girl found a gold ring and put it in a box with a small snake for safekeeping. When she returned both the ring and snake had grown. Terrified, she threw them into Lögurinn. The snake grew into the Lagarfljótsormur monster, threatening all who crossed the lake.

felling of previous eras. The **arboretum** has examples of around 70 tree species from around the world, all of which are well labelled. There are marked trails here for hikes or horseriding.

25 ▶ At 1,833m (6,012ft), **Mt Snæfell** is Iceland's highest peak outside the glacial zones. Although it last erupted some 10,000 years ago, geologists believe that it's still technically active. There are marker posts up the western side of the mountain showing the easiest route to the top, although you need to be experienced to tackle the peak itself. However, there are plenty of easier walks on the mountain, and there is the added attraction of the many reindeer that inhabit the area.

A river running through Hallormsstaður forest

The Eastfjords

Although the inlets along the east of Iceland are less dramatic than those in the west and north, they are dotted with lovely little villages, most of which are easily accessible from the ring road. Travellers arriving in Iceland by ferry normally dock at **Seyðisfjörður**, a pretty little ◀ **26** port surrounded by high mountains. A dirt road up to Mt Bjófur gives spectacular views down over the town and the fjord. The harbour area and Old Town, with its brightly painted wooden houses, is a good spot simply to wander. The town's **Bláa kirkjan** (Blue Church) organises classical concerts on Wednesday evenings from July to mid-August, and on Thursday (the day the ferry leaves) there is a craft market in town.

Kids at Lögurinn lake

From May to mid-September, boat trips sail from **Neskaupstaður** around the headland into near-deserted **Mjóifjörður**, past the highest sea-cliff in Iceland.

Eskifjörður is a busy fishing village with a large trawler fleet and a fish-freezing plant. **Sjóminjasafn** (Maritime Museum, Strandgata 39b; June–Aug daily 1–5pm; charge) is packed with boats, models, nets and fishing equipment. Just south of here, on a tall headland, is the **Hólmaborgir nature reserve**, where there are easy walks up to the summit.

The hills around the small fishing port of **Reyðarfjörður** have been worn flat by the now-vanished glaciers. The town was a naval base in World War II, and there is a museum, **Stríðsárasafnið** (Icelandic Wartime Museum, Austurvegur; June–Aug daily 1–6pm; charge), which documents the billeting of 3,000 Allied soldiers on the village in World War II.

A trip out from **Djúpivogur** to the uninhabited island of **Papey**, 'Monk's Island', reveals Iceland's smallest church – little bigger than a hen coop – which is chained to the ground to prevent it blowing away. Today the island is a nature reserve, home to seabirds (including 30,000 puffin pairs) and a large breeding colony of eider ducks.

THE WEST FJORDS

Travellers in the West Fjords face some of the worst roads in the country and the often inhospitable climate means it is a relatively little-visited part of Iceland. Yet the region offers Iceland's most dramatic, craggy fjords and some of its best hiking, while soaring cliffs host literally millions of breeding sea birds.

Ísafjörður and Around

27 The only town of any real size in the region is **Ísafjörður**. The deep harbour has helped it to become a major trading centre as well as an important fishing community. For a taste of just how tough an industry it can be, visit the **West Fjords Heritage Museum** (Sudurtangi; July–Aug Mon–Fri 10am–6pm, Sat–Sun 10am–5pm; June Mon–Fri 10am–5pm, Sat–Sun 1–5pm; charge). Housed in a well-restored timber warehouse,

Taking to the water near Ísafjörður

exhibits trace the development of the town and its fishing industry, with all sorts of unusual nautical paraphernalia. The town has a swimming pool, cinema and a few restaurants and hotels.

About 12km (7 miles) north, **Bolungarvík** is an exposed spot, liable to landslides and avalanches. It has a couple of little museums.

Arctic fox

The **Ósvör Maritime Museum** (June–mid-Aug daily 10am–5pm; charge) is in a restored fishing station and the **Natural History Museum** (Aðalstræti 21; June–mid-Aug Mon–Fri 9am–noon and 1–5pm; charge) has a jumble of stuffed animals including a seal and polar bear. Further west, the coast is largely uninhabited; the scenery is wild and imposing, a mixture of wind-lashed headlands and mighty snow-capped peaks.

Southeast of Ísafjörður, the road winds around several fjords to the village of **Reykjanes**, which is worth a stop for its heated outdoor pool and sauna. If you want to get close to a glacier, continue towards the **Kaldalón glacial lagoon**. From the head of the lagoon you can follow a walking trail for about an hour and a half to the tip of the glacier.

The area further north towards the **Hornstrandir Peninsula** is now uninhabited, after the last family left it in 1995. The beauty of this part of the country, with its sandy bays, rugged cliffs, meadows of wild flowers and massive bird colonies, is astonishing. For serious hiking it's hard to beat, and you can literally walk all day without meeting anyone. If you're lucky you might spot an Arctic fox and, offshore, whales and seals.

28

Dynjandi falls

West of Ísafjörður, the road runs through some tiny fishing villages as it heads south. There is a breath-taking descent into **Hrafn-seyri**, the birthplace of the Independence leader, Jón Sigurðsson. A small museum is dedicated to his memory (daily June–Aug 10am–8pm; charge), and there is much celebration in the village on Independence Day, 17 June. The **Dynjandi waterfall**, meaning 'the thundering one', just south of here, is a spectacular collection of cascades.

Tálknafjörður, to the west, is a lively spot. It has a pool, bike-hire shop, an adventure centre offering watersports and walking, and even a bar. Just outside town there is an open-air geothermal hotpot at **Stóri-Laugardalur**.

At **Látrabjarg**, you are at the most westerly point in Europe. What makes the long journey worthwhile are the amazing **bird cliffs** just outside the village. Thousands of puffins nest here in burrows, and you can get surprisingly close to them. There are at least as many guillemots, too, plus the largest colony of razorbills in the world. Although the noise the birds make can be deafening, the sight is unforgettable.

There is a wonderful **beach** at nearby **Rauðasandur**, with pink sand and superb surf thundering in from the Atlantic. **Hnjótur** is home to the **Egill Ólafsson Museum** (late-May–mid-Sept daily 10am–6pm; charge) with an odd-ball collection of marine rescue equipment, old telephones and a typewriter with Icelandic characters. The pride exhibit is a rusting Aeroflot biplane that ended up in Iceland after its pilot, fleeing Russia, was refused permission to land in the US. Outside is a replica Viking longship, a gift from Norway to mark 1,100 years of settlement.

THE WEST COAST

The stretch of coastline south from the West Fjords to Reykjavík is often passed through quickly by visitors on their way to other parts. However, two things in particular bring visitors to the peninsula: the extinct volcano, **Snæfellsjökull**, and **whale-watching** tours from Ólafsvík.

The Snæfellsnes Peninsula
At 1,445m (4,740ft) high **Snæfellsjökull** is permanently snow-capped. It was made famous worldwide by Jules Verne

Fishing fleet at Stykkishólmur harbour

A breathtaking view from Snæfellsjökull

as the entry point for his *Journey to the Centre of the Earth* and also plays a role in *Under the Glacier*, by Nobel Prize-winning Icelandic novelist Halldór Laxness. The glacier is popular for snowmobile tours. The main peak itself is a less daunting climb than it looks, but only experienced climbers should try it, as the weather is always a danger here.

Whale-watching tours (twice daily June–Aug; book with Sæferðir, tel: 438 1450) leave **Ólafsvík** by catamaran. This is a good place to spot killer whales, humpbacks and, if you're lucky, the massive blue whale.

Further north, **Stykkishólmur** is an attractive place with brightly painted wooden houses down by the harbour. The town is famous for its scallops and halibut. At the quayside it's possible to take a two-hour birdwatching and scallop-tasting tour. There is an unusual modern **church** overlook-ing the town and decorated with hundreds of brightly .uminated bulbs suspended from the ceiling. Classical music ..certs take place on Sundays in summer (charge). South of the town, the mountain of **Helgafell**, much talked about in Icelandic folklore, is not much more than a hillock. But it is said you can have three wishes granted if you climb it from the west in silence and then descend to the east without looking back.

Stykkishólmur is the best place to get a car/passenger ferry out to the delightful island of **Flatey**. It's a sleepy, peaceful ◄ 30 little place, with restored wooden houses set among bright yellow fields of buttercups. The eastern part of the island is a **nature reserve** teeming with birdlife. Watch out for the Arctic tern, which seem particularly aggressive here – even the island's sheep aren't immune from their dive-bombing attacks. There is a fine little church, which was painted by the Catalan artist Baltasar in return for free accommodation, and, next door, the oldest and smallest library in Iceland. You can stay overnight in summer, but in winter the island is virtually deserted.

Reykholt and Vicinity

Both its setting and its cultural history make **Reykholt** a ◄ 31 place worth visiting. The wide open spaces of its valley setting are refreshing after so many mountains, and this also was the home of Snorri Sturluson, born in 1179 and immortalised by his saga-writing. He was a distinguished scholar but was murdered here in 1241 after falling foul of the Norwegian king. You can visit **Snorralaug**, the bathing pool where the chieftain would receive visitors and,

Beacon on cliffs

Tumbling falls of Hraunfossar

beside it, the partly-restored remains of a tunnel that led to his farmhouse. There a fine museum about Sturluson in the **Heimskringla Exhibition Hall** (May–Sept daily 10am–6pm, Oct–Apr Mon–Fri 9am–5pm; charge), located just next to the church.

At **Húsafell**, to the east, many Icelanders have holiday cottages. There is access from here to a forest and two **glaciers**, Okjökull and Eiríksjökull, as well as a long **lava cave** at Hallmundarhraun. Nearby is the magnificent **Hraunfossar**, a multitude of tiny cascades that tumble into the Hvíta River along a 1km (½-mile) stretch.

Further north is the reconstructed farmhouse of **Eiríksstaðir** (June–Aug daily 9am–6pm; charge; www.leif.is), from which the Vikings launched their westward voyages of discovery. Erík the Red, after whom the farm is named, went on to discover Greenland, while his son, Leifur, was the first European to set foot in America. There is a reconstruction of the original farm, complete with Viking guides, next to the excavated hall; the latter dates from 890–980.

Borgarnes

32 ▶ **Borgarnes**, on the windswept west coast route south to Reykjavík, is essentially a service centre for the neighbouring dairy farms. The park, known as **Skallagrímsgarður**, commemorates one of Iceland's first settlers, Skallagrímur Kveldúlfsson, whose burial mound is still visible. His son, Egill, was the hero of *Egill's Saga*, and there is a monument to him by the mound. **The Settlement Centre of Iceland** (daily June–Aug 10am–7pm, Sept–May 11am–5pm; charge) is a striking new multimedia exhibition housed in a restored warehouse by the harbour. It uses the sagas to explore Iceland's early history and half of the centre is dedicated to Eigill.

A short distance north is **Borg á Myrum**, nothing more than a large rock beside a church, where Skallagrímur and his family lived. There is a **statue** by Ásmundur Sveinsson commemorating the poem Egill wrote about the death of his son. The writer Snorri Sturluson *(see page 83)*, who is thought to have written *Egill's Saga*, also lived here.

Akranes

Sturdy Icelandic horse

Located just north of Reykjavík, **Akranes** is dominated by fish-processing, trawler production and cement making. Far more appealing is the **Safnasvæðið á Akranesi** (Akranes Folk Museum; daily June–Aug 10am–5pm, Sept–May 1–5pm; charge), east of town. It houses a folk museum with the emphasis on maritime history, including a well-preserved ketch, one of the first decked fishing boats in Iceland. There is also the country's largest collection of rocks, minerals and fossils. There are swimming pools and four hotpots adjacent on Garðar.

Jets of steam and hot-water pools at Hveravellir

THE INTERIOR

Iceland's barren interior – a place so desolate that the Apollo astronauts came here to train for their moon landing – can be crossed by two main north–south routes: the Kjölur (F35, also known as the Kjalvegur) and Sprengisandur (F26), both of which are open only once the snow has melted in summer; some of the more minor routes remain closed throughout the summer if conditions are poor. The weather is generally very unpredictable here, so always go prepared for the worst.

Camping is the only form of accommodation, apart from a few huts operated by Ferðafélag Íslands (Touring Club of Iceland, tel: 568 2533). Visitors without transport can take advantage of the scheduled buses that run between Reykjavík and Akureyri via the Kjölur route (daily in July and August) and between Reykjavík and Lake Mývatn via Sprengisandur (twice weekly from mid-July to late August).

The Kjölur Route

Comparatively straightforward to drive, the Kjölur is the most popular crossing through the central highlands. This is the only route through the interior that travellers could consider making in a normal car, although it is still very strongly advisable to travel by four-wheel drive.

Based on an ancient byway used in saga times, it runs from Gullfoss to the Blöndudalur Valley, passing between the Langjökull and Hofsjökull ice-caps. Behind Gullfoss, the River Hvítá flows out of Hvítárvatn, a glacial lake at the foot of Langjökull. From the main route you should be able to see the lake and its glacial spurs, which extend up to its shores.

The route soon reaches its highest point (just over 670m/ 2,200ft), where a memorial stone commemorates the achievements of Geir Zoëga, an engineer who was for many years in charge of building Iceland's roads.

At the centre of the Kjölur plateau, is **Hveravellir**, an extraordinary area of intense geothermal activity, with hot springs, a hot pool where you can bathe, camping facilities and good overnight huts. Also at Hveravellir is a modest stone shelter where the bandit Fjalla Eyvindur and his wife Halla spent a whole winter in hiding in the 18th century.

The northern section of the route, which is less attractive, follows a new track through the reservoir basin created for Blönduvirkjun hydroelectric power station. After crossing the Blanda River at about halfway between Blönduós and Varmahlíð, you will reach the Blöndudalur Valley and then the ring road.

Cauldron on Kjölur plateau

The Sprengisandur Route

The second main crossing through the interior, the Sprengisandur route, runs from the Bárðardalur Valley between Akureyri and Lake Mývatn to Þjórsá, east of Selfoss. It is accessible by four-wheel drive only and covers some of the most desolate ground in the country.

There are three main ways to reach the start of the route proper, all of which converge at or near Laugafell at the edge of the Sprengisandur. The most easterly way (route 842 then F26) heads through the Bárðardalur Valley via two waterfalls: Goðafoss and the basalt Aldeyjarfoss. A more central route (F821) goes from the end of the Eyjafjörður Valley, past the former farm/weather station at Nýibær, towards Laugafell. The third, most westerly, route (F752) meanders through the Vesturdalur Valley, from Skagafjörður, towards the wet grasslands of Orravatnsrústir and Austari Jökulsá, a huge glacial river fed by the Hofsjökull glacier.

At Laugafell, on a ridge leading northwest from the mountain of the same name, there are several warm springs, a warm bathing pool and a tourist hut. Nearby, the gravel expanse of the Sprengisandur begins with magnificent vistas east to Vatnajökull and the smaller Tungnafellsjökull and west to Hofsjökull. A number of river crossings later, the blue tongues of glaciers come into view. A track forking to the east leads off the gravel plain to Gæsavötn, a small yellow-green oasis and crystal-clear lake amid the dark dramatic landscape. Beyond lie the Gæsavatnaleið and Askja routes.

Bathing in natural hot springs

The rhyolitic hills of the interior

At Nýidalur, close to the geographical centre of Iceland is a small campsite, on the only patch of green in the area, and several huts. The next stop on the route is shortly after the mountain of Kistualda (790m/2,600ft). The dusty track south to **Þórisvatn**, Iceland's second largest lake, continues the landscape of glaciers and black gravel plains. Just beyond the lake is the tiny settlement of Hrauneyjafoss, where there is a petrol station, coffee-shop and small guesthouse.

Next is **Landmannalaugar**, part of the Fjallabak Nature Reserve and a good base for the many walks in the area (there are camping and hut facilities here). Landmannalaugar's spectacular rhyolitic hills are bright yellow, green and red, dotted with deep blue lakes. There are hot springs here, and steam rises from every corner of the valley.

From Landmannalaugar, it is possible either to head southwestwards to meet the ring road near the south coast or southeast to Bláfjall and the coast.

WHAT TO DO

OUTDOOR ACTIVITIES

There is a great deal on offer for exploring the great outdoors in Iceland, from gentle hikes and horse-riding excursions to more demanding pursuits such as ice-climbing and white-water rafting.

Walking and Hiking

There are hiking trails throughout Iceland to suit every level. The more ambitious routes require some previous experience and a high level of fitness. The weather can change unexpectedly and if you can't read a map and a compass properly then don't attempt the hikes that take you away from populated areas. However, even for the inexperienced there are some great walks. For advice on safety, protecting the environment and routes in national parks, the best source of information is the **Iceland Nature Conservation Association** (Hringbraut 121, 107 Reykjavík, tel: 551 2279, www.inca.is).

The two organisations that provide information as well as offering guided hikes and details of mountain huts for overnight stays are: **Ferðafélag Íslands** (Touring Club of Iceland, Mörkinni 6, 108 Reykjavík, tel: 568 2533, www.fi.is) and **Útivist** (Laugavegi 178, 105 Reykjavík, tel: 562 1000, www.utivist.is). Tourist offices can provide maps and local contacts for guides.

By far the best months for hiking are June, July and August, when the weather is relatively warm, and visibility is at its best. Beginners could start with some of the excellent walking tours of Reykjavík, including the **Seltjarnarnes-Heiðmörk Pathway**. Suggested routes, which vary from one to six hours in duration, are available from tourist offices.

Spectacular hiking country

Every part of the country has its trails. Some of the best areas for walking and hiking include:

Þingvellir National Park. Marked trails around historic sites and lakeland. One option is a full-day hike up Mt Armannsfell.

Þórsmörk Trail. Routes from the relatively gentle to the challenging. There is access to glaciers in this area.

Snæfellsnes Peninsula. A rugged and often wet area. Ascent of the glacier for experienced hikers.

Hornstrandir. One of the wildest and most isolated parts of the country, suitable for the experienced only.

Lake Mývatn. Flat and gentle routes amid terrific scenery.

Jökulsárgljúfur National Park. Well-marked trails at all levels taking from a few hours to four days.

Mt Snæfell. Demanding hikes from Egilsstaðir along the lake and up the mountain.

Lónsöræfi Reserve. A dozen or so tracks close to the immense Vatnajökull glacier.

Hikes into the **interior**, where there are few roads and no villages, can be very tough but rewarding. The mighty rivers make many of the routes and tracks unpassable by foot, but the F35 Kjölur track is passable in summer without a vehicle. Always seek advice from one of the touring organisations (*see page 91*) before setting off.

Horse Riding

There have been horses in Iceland for as long as there have been people in the country. They are used for farming and riding and can be hired, with or without guides, from farms and activity centres all over Iceland. You can do treks of up to 10 days, with accommodation in tents or huts. If you are bringing your own equipment or clothing it must be disinfected on arrival. There are many companies organising horse riding and treks; one of the best is eco-travel company, **Íshestar** (Sörlaskeið 26, 220 Hafnarfjörður, tel: 555 7000, www.ishestar.is). The magazine *Eiðfaxi International* (www.eidfaxi.is) is published for Icelandic horse lovers worldwide.

Fishing

Salmon and trout fishing in Iceland has an international reputation. Free from industrial pollution, Iceland's waterways are prime habitats for wild fish, and give the chance of outstanding catches. For salmon the season is from around the third week of June until mid-September varying slightly according to region, and for trout it's April/May until late September/October, depending on the location. Excellent fishing is available but at a very high price, which varies according to river and facilities available. Permits can cost an incredible ISK15,000–100,000 per day, and sometimes even more. The other snag is that most rivers have to be booked months, if not years, in advance. For further information contact the **National Angling Association** (Bændahöllin, Hagatorg, 107 Reykjavík, tel: 553 1510, www.angling.is).

Iceland sits in the North Atlantic's best fishing grounds. Sea angling has traditionally been considered an industry rather than a pastime, but it is now also becoming popular as a sport. The season begins in late May and runs until the end of August. Contact **Angling Club Lax-á** (Akurhvarf 16, 203 Kópavogur, tel: 557 6100, www.lax-a.net).

Birdwatching

The quantity and variety of bird life in Iceland has really to be seen to be believed and is home to some of of the largest breeding colonies in the world. You will find birds all over the country, along the coast and in the mountains, but the best locations are:

Látrabjarg in the West Fjords: the largest bird cliff known in the world, including the biggest colony of razorbills anywhere on earth.

Heimaey: the site of Iceland's largest puffin colony.

Lake Mývatn, in the north: there are more species of breeding ducks here than anywhere in Europe.

Dyrhólaey Cliffs and elsewhere along the south coast has

Iceland's Birdlife

Iceland's exposed northern location means that while as many as 350 species of birds come here every year, relatively few breed, although recent warming of the climate has increased this number. Sea-birds make up the majority, with as many as 13 million breeding pairs. The puffin population alone rises to more than 10 million by late summer. There are also large numbers of waders and wildfowl. Many species are strictly protected by law.

The lesser black-backed gull is the first migrant to arrive, in February/March, but the locals regard the arrival of the golden plover in April as the start of spring. The best time to go birdwatching is in early summer. Many breeds pass through during the last two weeks of May on their way north to Greenland. In early June the resident breeding species begin their mating rituals. It's important not to disturb the birds at this time. In the second half of June the chicks start to hatch and by mid-August they are leaving the nest. While a few breeds migrate to Iceland for the winter, there is not much to see and puffins, for example, will have gone in search of warmer climes.

Arctic tern as well as the world's largest skua colony. The **Icelandic Society for the Protection of Birds** can be contacted at PO Box 5069, 125 Reykjavík, tel: 562 0477, www.fuglavernd.is/index.php/eng.

Ice-climbing and Glacier Walks

In summer guided day-walks on the glaciers from Skaftafell (part of the Vatnajökull National Park) can be arranged with two groups based at the visitor centre: the **Icelandic Mountain Guides** (tel: 894 2959, 478 2559, www.mountain guide.is) and newcomers the **Glacier Guides** (tel: 659 7000, www.glacierguides.is). For more ambitious expeditions contact the **Icelandic Alpine Club** (Íslenski Alpaklúbburinn, Skutuvógur 1G, 104 Reykjavík; tel: 868 8754; e-mail: info@isalp.is; www.isalp.is) for information before setting out, and, once you are ready to go, advise the club of your departure and return.

Glacier tours with **snowmobiles** are a safe and fun way to see the ice close up. The best take you on to the Vatnajökull glacier in the southeast and the Snæfellsjökull glacier in the west. Contact the **Activity Group** (Tunguháls 8, 110 Reykjavík, tel: 580 9900, www.activity.is)

Skiing is possible all year round

Snow Sports

Cross-country skiing has been a way of life in many parts of Iceland in the winter, although it's now starting to be developed as a tourist pursuit. **Downhill skiing** and **snowboarding** are increasingly popular. Bláfjöll, just outside Reykjavík, has five ski areas at different levels. In winter, however, the limited daylight makes skiing difficult, although night skiing excursions are available. Kerlingarfjöll, near the Hofsjökull glacier in the interior, has skiing all year round with a summer ski school, but book well in advance. There is good skiing at Akureyri, where the lifts range from 500–1,000m (1,640–3,280ft), with more basic runs at Ísafjörður, Eskifjörður, and Siglufjörður. The best time of year for this sport is around March and April. For up-to-date information tel: 462 2280. Many tour operators run skiing trips, or check with the Icelandic Alpine Club *(see page 95)*.

Dog-sledding is a great way to see Iceland's mountains and glaciers. **Dog Steam Tours** (tel: 487 7747, www.dogsledding.is) offers different excursions, on snow or glaciers depending on conditions.

White-Water Rafting

Although this is a relatively new sport in Iceland, it is steadily growing in popularity. The water can be very cold, but you will be provided with all the right gear to protect you from its effects. There is a minimum age, which depends on the risk level. Among the companies organising trips are **Activity Tours**, based in the north near Sauðárkrókur (560 Varmahlíð, tel: 453 8383, www.rafting.is) and the Activity Group *(see page 95 for contact details)*.

Speeding on the Skálafellsjökull

Swimming

More than just a sport in Iceland, swimming is a social activity for all the family,

Iceland offers great opportunities for whale-watching

and there are geothermally heated pools in most towns and many villages. If you want to do serious lengths, the best pool in Reykjavík is at Laugardalur on Sundlaugavegur (tel: 553 4039; Mon–Fri 6.50am–10pm, Sat–Sun 8am–10pm; charge). It has a 50m (160ft) pool, three hot pots, a Jacuzzi, steam room, sun lamps and waterslide. Swimming costumes can be hired for a small fee.

Whale-Watching

Whale-watching started in Iceland as recently as 1995, but since then the number of companies offering tours has been increasing all the time. There's a good chance of seeing at least something – most likely the common minke whale, although humpbacks, fin and even blue whales are spotted from time to time, as well as dolphins and porpoises. If you don't see anything at all, most companies will offer you a free second trip.

Golf at Vestmannaeyjar

There are departures from Reykjavík, Keflavík, Stykkishólmur, Ólafsvík, Heimaey, Dalvík, and Húsavík, where there is a Whale Museum. You don't have to be on a boat to see whales – just looking out to sea might reveal a whale's back breaking the surface.

Cycling

The unmade roads and high winds in much of Iceland can make cycle touring a challenge, to say the least. Off-road cycling is prohibited to help protect the environment.

The **Icelandic Mountain Bike Club** (Íslenski Fjallhjólaklúbburinn, PO Box 5193, 125 Reykjavík, tel: 562 0099, www.mmedia.is/~ifhk/tourist.htm) is a great source of advice and has suggested itineraries.

Golf

With 65 courses, golf is thriving in Iceland. Most courses have just nine holes, however there are fifteen 18-hole courses including those in: Reykjavík (Grafarholt and Korpa), Hafnarfjörður (Keilir), Garðabær (Oddur), Hella, Keflavík (Suðurnes), Vestmannaeyjar and Akureyri. For further information contact the **Golf Federation of Iceland** (Golfsamband Íslands, Engjavegur 6, Reykjavík, tel: 514 4050, www.golf.is). The major golfing event in Iceland is the Arctic Open, which takes place in June each year and is open to professional and amateur golfers alike. Hosts to the event are the **Akureyri Golf Club** (600 Akureyri, tel: 462 2974, www.arcticopen.is).

SHOPPING

Shopping in Iceland was not high on the travel agenda for most tourists because prices were considered ridiculously high, but things have changed. Although the 2008 economic crisis was atrocious news for Icelanders, today's weak króna means that tourists can buy Icelandic goods at reduced rates, at least compared to those of a few short years ago.

In the centre of Reykjavík, most of the tourist shops are in and around Hafnarstræti and Austurstræti, though Laugavegur, leading out of the centre, is home to the majority of the fashion shops (there is an excellent bookshop at No. 18, Mál & Menning, with almost an entire floor given over to titles in English) and Skólavörðustígur, which branches off Laugavegur at a sharp diagonal, is good for gifts and crafts. In the suburbs are two large malls, Smáralind and Kringlan, which house most of the usual European high-street chain stores. The biggest, Kringlan, has 150 shops and is easy to reach – it's just a 15-minute bus-ride from the city centre.

For **souvenirs** try Icelandic woollen sweaters, gloves, scarves and hats. Most are produced by small workshops and come in all shapes, sizes and colours. The Handknitting As-

Tax-Free Shopping

It's worth remembering that on departure from Iceland you can get a refund of the VAT (Value Added Tax) paid on goods over ISK4,000 provided they were purchased in the previous three months. The shop assistant will fill out a Tax Free form – keep this safe, along with your purchase receipt. If the total is more than ISK5,000, you will have to show the goods themselves on your way out of the country, otherwise just the receipts will do. This does not apply for woollen goods. This scheme can save you up to 15 percent on the price of many items.

Woollen goods on display

sociation of Iceland's shop (Handþrjónasamband Íslands, Skólavörðustigur 19, tel: 552 1890) has a wide selection. The same street has a number of **art** galleries selling some excellent local work, as well as **craft shops** for handicrafts, stones and other minerals. Duvets, quilts and other bedcovers are also very good quality, although those filled with locally gathered eider down can be expensive.

For traditional **Icelandic music**, try the album Íslensk alþýðulög (Icelandic Folk Songs). There are also fine classical recordings by the Iceland Symphony Orchestra, particularly of works by late composer Jón Leifs. Of course, Björk and Sigur Rós are Iceland's biggest musical exports, but the modern music scene is ever-changing and new bands appear all the time.

Smoked salmon, roe caviar, dried fish and *skyr*, a delicious Icelandic yoghurt, are good food buys, but be aware of the import restrictions

NIGHTLIFE

Since the early 1990s Reykjavík at night has been transformed from a sleepy provincial city to one of the hottest venues in Europe, with as lively a nightlife – in the bars and clubs clustered in the tiny city centre.

There are dozens of very welcoming bars and cafés for a drink or light meal during the evening, but the serious clubbing doesn't start until well after midnight. Icelanders tend to dress up a bit to go out, and there can be long queues outside the most fashionable places on Friday and Saturday. As with most cities, clubs and pubs open and close in Reykjavík all the time, so it's worth asking around to find out where the newest and most fashionable places are. The publication *What's On in Reykjavík* is a good starting point. Some of the best pubs and clubs that have been around for some time include Café Victor (Hafnarstræti 1–3), Kaffi Reykjavík (Vesturgata 2), Nasa (Austurvöllur) and Hverfisbarinn (Hverfisgata 20).

For more **cultural** nights out, Reykjavík has its own ballet, opera, symphony orchestra and several theatre and dance groups. *What's On in Reykjavík* and local papers list the latest shows. Jazz venues include Kaffileikhúsið (Café Theatre, Vesturgata 3) and the restaurant Jazz at Jómfrúin (Læk-

Reykjavík has a good selection of stylish bars

jargata 4), which has jazz recitals in summer (Sat 4–6pm).

Outside the capital nightlife can be hard to find, although Akureyri is becoming increasingly popular. Góði Dátinn (Geislagata 14, Akureyri) is packed with a young crowd on Friday and Saturday and often has live bands.

ACTIVITIES FOR CHILDREN

Icelanders try to involve children in almost all their sporting and cultural activities. Swimming and horse riding are particularly popular with local children, and families gather in large numbers at weekends to feed the ducks and geese at Tjörn in front of City Hall.

The pool at Laugardalur *(see page 97)* has a huge 85m (280ft) waterslide and a children's pool. At the same site, Reykjavík's Zoo and Family Park (daily 10am–6pm, until 5pm in winter; admission charge, free for under-fives, www.mu.is) is always a hit with the kids, and when they tire of looking at the seals, foxes, reindeer, horses, cows, pigs and all the other animals, they can head for the Family Park and climb a replica Viking ship and cross a man-made lake on a

Brown cow

raft. There is a large grill that can be used free of charge for barbecuing. The seals are fed twice a day (11am and 4pm).

For older children there are two bowling rinks, Keiluhöllin at Öskjuhlíð (Sun–Tue noon–midnight, Fri–Sat noon–2am) and Keila at Mjódd (Mon–Fri noon–11.30pm, Sat–Sun 10am–11.30pm).

Calendar of Events

Precise dates of events change from year to year as they are linked to religious holidays or the seasons. Check with tourist offices for details.

6 January Twelfth Night, marked with songs, bonfires and fireworks.

Late January Þorri. The half-way point of winter, this festival involves eating delicacies including lambs' heads and testicles and cured shark.

Early February Festival of Lights. Reykjavík's winter festival with arts and cultural events.

Ash Wednesday A children's carnival ends three days of events. Cream buns are consumed on 'Bun Day', the Monday, followed by enormous meat dishes on Tuesday, 'Bursting Day'.

End of April The First Day of Summer. Children's events in most towns, with parades, fairs and flag days.

1st Sunday in June Festival of the Sea. Celebrations in all coastal communities with sports and dances.

17 June National Day. Formal ceremonies in the morning and partying and fairs all afternoon and evening.

Late June Akureyri Theatre Festival. Street artists, puppet shows and major productions.

Early July Landsmót National Horse Show, Skagafjörður.

Late July Week-long Whale Festival, Húsavík.

1st Monday in August Summer Bank Holiday. A long weekend for all Icelanders, with open-air pop festivals around the country.

3rd Saturday in August Reykjavík's birthday celebrations with cultural events of all kinds. The City Marathon is held on the same day.

September/October Reykjavík Film Festival featuring both Icelandic and international movies.

Late October Iceland Airwaves. A four-day contemporary music event.

23 December St Þorláksmessa. Traditional feasts mark one of Iceland's few indigenous saints and the high point of the pre-Christmas celebrations.

31 December New Year's Eve. A satirical revue on television, followed by outdoor parties that can last all night.

EATING OUT

Dining out in Iceland has undergone tremendous changes in the past 20 years. Many Icelandic chefs have sought training abroad, then returned home to apply their new-found gourmet knowledge to traditional ingredients. The restaurant scene has been hit by a great wave of energy, enthusiasm and experimentation, and dining out in Reykjavík is consequently a real treat. Prices are not low in Iceland's better restaurants – but you are paying for excellent meals made with high-quality ingredients.

Iceland was effectively cut off from the rest of Europe for centuries, and, with very little in the way of food imports, no Icelandic *haute cuisine* developed. The population depended on what they could catch or grow themselves, making do with a diet based almost entirely on fish, lamb and vegetables such as potatoes. Various methods were devised to preserve the food so it could be used for months after it was caught. Meat was smoked, salted and pickled. Fish

Meal Times

Icelanders tend to have their main meal in the middle of the day and this is also when you can find some of the better priced all-inclusive menus (often restricted to around noon–2.30pm). In Reykjavík and many of the larger towns, restaurants tend to be open all day from about 11.30am until 11pm (later at weekends), so you don't have to be too organised about when you eat. In some smaller places, cafés and restaurants shut at about 2.30pm and reopen around 7pm. They close anytime after 10pm, so it's always a good idea to check their opening times before planning your evening. Breakfast hours are relaxed, so you don't usually have to be up too early to fit in with them.

Fresh fish is a staple in Iceland

would be hung out and dried, or smoked in dung or salted, or even buried. You will still occasionally see fish-drying racks on the hillsides as you drive around the country.

Traditional Foods

The two staple foods are fish and lamb. Fish is most plentiful and cheaper, so every meal, from breakfast onwards, will usually include it in some form. Wind-dried cod or haddock, *harðfiskur,* is a popular snack. It's torn into strips, beaten to soften it and eaten with butterr, accompanied with a glass of milk or maybe something stronger.

Whalemeat *(hval),* mostly from minke whales, is commonly found on menus, to the consternation of some tourists. It is usually soaked first in milk to extract some of the oil, and then served as medallions or steaks. It tends to be an expensive meat product due to the high costs associated with whaling.

Long-life larder

Ice-covered land and frozen seas forced Icelanders to preserve their fish and meat, so it could be stored and eaten throughout winter.

One of Iceland's most notorious food rituals is the ceremonious intake of rotten shark *(hákarl)* and schnapps. After being buried for three months or more, shark becomes acrid and ammoniac; rubbery and rotten, it is washed down in small cubes with ample quantities of the Icelandic spirit, *brennivín*.

Most Icelandic seafood, by contrast, is absolutely delicious and comes to your plate very fresh indeed. Icelandic cod, halibut, turbot and monkfish, for example, are juicy and succulent. Salmon and trout from the rivers are large and relatively inexpensive, as is char, a species of trout that is found all over Iceland. Smoked salmon and gravadlax (smoked salmon marinated with herbs) are both of very high quality.

While you will never go short of tasty fish, you might tire of it after a while. The other Icelandic staple, lamb, may cost more, but the taste is exceptional. Sheep farms on the island are small, and the flocks are allowed to graze wild in the highlands, where they eat herbs as well as grass. As a result, the meat has quite a gamey flavour.

As with fish, lamb was traditionally smoked to produce *hangikjöt,* which is eaten hot or cold. Nothing was ever allowed to go to waste in winter in Iceland, and dishes made of sheep's offal are still produced. *Slátur* (literally: slaughter) is a haggis-like dish made from all manner of left-overs, pressed into cakes, pickled in whey and cooked in stomach lining. Alternatively *svið* are boiled and singed sheep's heads, minus the brains, that are eaten either fresh or pickled. The meat is sometimes then taken off the bone and pressed to produce *sviðasulta.* A real delicacy, served on special occasions, is *súrsaðir hrútspungar* (pickled rams' testicles).

A limited amount of game finds its way on to the dinner plate. Reindeer from the east of the country is similar to venison. Ptarmigan is a grouse-like bird and a favourite at Christmas time. Icelanders are quite happy to eat their national symbol, too: puffin is often seen on the menu; it is frequently smoked and produces quite a dark, rich meat.

The main locally produced vegetables are potatoes and turnips. Wild berries are often used in sauces and puddings, and rhubarb thrives in the cold climate. Otherwise the dessert course is often cakes or pastries. One delicious treat is *skyr,* a yoghurt-type dish made of pasteurised skimmed milk and live bacteria; it's often mixed with fruit flavouring and is high in calcium and low in calories.

Bread, often made with rye, is a normal accompaniment to any meal. It may be baked in underground ovens in the naturally hot earth to produce *hverabrauð* ('steam bread').

Café Riis in Holmavík *(see page 114)* serves up delicious meals

Beer ban

Drinking beer was illegal in Iceland from 1915–89. Its reintroduction – on 1 March 1989 – is celebrated annually as *Bjórdagurinn* Beer Day).

Rye pancakes, known as *flatkaka*, go well with smoked salmon and other *smorgasbord*-type toppings.

What to Drink

Not surprisingly, the Icelandic climate is not conducive to wine-growing, so all wines are imported and therefore extremely expensive.

Traditionally, drinking alcohol mid-week has not been part of Icelandic culture, although it is becoming more common to have a glass of wine or beer with a meal when dining out. A strong Protestant work ethic is usually cited as the cause… along with the inflated price of alcohol. The bottle that is expensive enough at the state liquor store *(vínbúðar)* will invariably be around three times higher in price at a restaurant. Even house wines generally cost around ISK600–1,000 per glass, and a decent bottle of wine in a good restaurant will cost upwards of ISK5,000. Beer, whilst not exactly inexpensive, is generally a more affordable ISK700 per half litre.

Icelandic spirits, on the other hand, are both strong and tasty. *Brennivín* ('burnt wine') is a schnapps distilled from potatoes and flavoured with caraway seeds. Its nickname is 'Black Death', which gives an idea of its strength. A good variant is *Hvannarótar*, which is flavoured with angelica.

Coffee is the national drink of Iceland, consumed from early morning to late at night, at home, at work or even walking down the street. Refills are usually included if you buy a cup of standard coffee in a café, and some petrol stations have a free jug on the counter for their petrol-buying customers. In recent years, there has been a veritable explosion in the coffee culture in Iceland and it's now possible to get expertly brewed espressos, cappuccinos and lattes.

MENU READER

Gætum við/get ég fengið...   Could we/I have...

Basics

ávextir	fruit
bakað	baked
baunir	peas, beans
brauð	bread
glóðað	grilled
grænmeti	vegetables
hrísgrjón	rice
kartöflur	potatoes
laukur	onion
ostar	cheeses
reykt	smoked
salat	salad
smjör	butter
smárettir	snacks
soðið	boiled
steikt	fried
súpa	soup

Drinks

appelsínusafi	orange juice
bjór	beer
kaffi	coffee
mjólk	milk
te	tea
vatn	water
vín	wine
(hrauðvín)	(red)
(hvítvín)	(white)

Fiskur (Fish)

bleikja	char
hörpuskel	scallop
humar	lobster
lax	salmon
lúða	halibut
rauðspretta	plaice
sandhverfa	turbot
síld	herring
siltungur	trout
skötuselur	monkfish
steinbítur	catfish
ýsa	haddock
rækja	shrimp
þorskur	cod

Kjöt (Meat)

kjúklingur	chicken
lambakjöt	lamb
lambakótelettur	lamb chop
lundi	puffin
nautakjöt	beef
nautalundir	beef fillet
nautasteik	beef steak
skinka	ham
svínakjöt	pork
lítið steikt	rare
miðlungs steikt	med
vel steikt	

PLACES TO EAT

We have used the following symbols to give an idea of the price for a three-course meal for one, excluding wine:

$$$$ over ISK10,000	**$$** ISK2,500–5,000
$$$ ISK5,000–10,000	**$** belo0w ISK2,500

REYKJAVÍK

Á Næstu Grösum $ *Laugavegur 20B, tel: 552 8410.* Delicious, wholesome vegetarian food, an airy, relaxed atmosphere and good value for money make this a very popular place, particularly at lunch time. Indian theme on Fridays; lunch not served on Sunday. The entrance is on Klapparstigúr.

Apótek Bar-Grill $$$ *Austurstræti 16, tel: 575 7900.* The kind of trendy place where you'll spot Reykjavík's young, fashionable people, who don't mind paying a bit over the odds. Located on the site of a former chemist – hence the name – Apótek is still a little clinical for some tastes. However, the food, especially the fish-based starters, is consistently good, and the menus are changed every four months to keep people coming back for more. Busy at weekends.

Dill $$$ *Nordic House, Sturlugata 5, tel: 552 1522.* A gourmet's delight, this elegant new Scandinavian restaurant specialises in local, organic ingredients cooked in contemporary 'Nordic Kitchen' style. Prepare yourself for mouthwatering dishes such as smoked haddock with blue mussels, reindeer with blueberry sauce, and almond cake with cinnamon ice-cream.

e Gallery Restaurant $$$$ *Bergstaðastræti 37, tel: 552* . The Gallery Restaurant is arguably the best restaurant in ital (inside Hotel Holt) with a magnificent display of Ice- rt. The chef uses fresh local produce, including a wide ꞵsh, reindeer and lamb, and presents the dishes with

Grænn Kostur $ *Skólavörðustígur 8, tel: 552 2028*. A terrific little vegetarian restaurant with great-value, wholesome food. There is a choice between two main courses of the day, although you can have a little of each, and the menu changes daily. The famed garlic and chilli sauce is always available. Delicious banana, apple and carrot cakes to finish off the meal.

Icelandic Fish & Chips $$ *Tryggvagata 8, tel: 511 1118*. The fish and chips here are given a healthy spin, made with organic potatoes and the freshest quality fish. No wheat or sugar is used in the fish batter, the chips are roasted rather than deep-fried, and the unusual selection of dressings is made using low-fat, yoghurt-like *skyr*. It does a roaring trade in takeaways, too.

Jómfrúin $ *Lækjargata 4, tel: 551 0100*. An excellent choice for lunch, when the restaurant is full with homesick Danes. A seemingly endless choice of filling Danish-style open sandwiches. Choose carefully and lunch need not cost more than ISK1,700.

Lækjarbrekka $$$ *Bankastræti 2, tel: 551 4430*. In an atmospheric timber building dating from 1834, this cosy restaurant with period furniture, chandeliers and heavy drapes is known for its gourmet set menus featuring lobster, puffin or lamb. It's an excellent choice for a special occasion. Finish off with a drink in the snug lounge upstairs.

Café Paris $$ *Austurstræti 14, tel: 551 1020*. A Reykjavík classic, this cosy little cafe overlooking Austurvöllur square and the Parliament Buildings, has been here as long as anyone can remember. Quintessentially Parisian in style and feel, this is a good choice for a light lunch and a good cup of coffee. In summer there is outdoor seating.

Primavera $$$ *Austurstræti 9, tel: 561 8555*. Come here top-class northern Italian cooking with sun-dried tom puréed mushrooms, polenta and balsamic vinegar fe strongly on the menu. There's a large, minimalist din on the first floor. The menu isn't extensive, but the quality is uniformly good.

Skólabrú $$$$ *Skólabrú 1, tel: 562 4455*. A stylishly chic restaurant mixing old-world charm with Nordic minimalism. Top-notch service and beautifully presented food. The menu has both Icelandic and international dishes, with an emphasis on seafood, duck and game.

Restaurant Silfur $$$$ *Pósthússtræti 11, tel: 551 1440*. Situated on the ground floor of Hotel Borg, this is certainly an elegant place surrounded by art deco splendour. Imagine that you are back in the 1930s – except, of course, for the distinctly modern day prices. The menu is eclectic and includes delights such as smoked puffin breast in a beetroot sauce.

Vegamót $$ *Vegamótastígur 4, tel: 511 3040*. An extremely popular bistro in the centre of town serving a varied menu of good-value food: everything from fresh fish to TexMex dishes. Plentiful brunch options are available until 4pm on Saturday and Sunday. It's also a relatively cheap place for a beer.

Við Tjörnina $$$ *Templarasund 3, tel: 551 8666*. Undoubtedly one of the city's finest fish restaurants located close to Tjörnin lake, as the Icelandic name suggests. A unique menu with creatively prepared fish which never fails to tantalise the tastebuds.

Þrir Frakkar $$ *Baldursgata 14, tel: 552 3939*. They've been serving whale steaks at this cosy neighbourhood French-style bistro for years and it's still the best place in town to sample the meat, should your conscience allow. Otherwise, an accomplished menu of fish dishes, including the traditional *plokkfiskur*, a kind of fish and potato mash, is on offer.

SOUTH AND SOUTHEAST

tel Skaftafell $$ *Freysnes, Skaftafell, tel: 478 1945*. riced meat and fish dishes are served every evening in-otel restaurant.

Hótel Geysir $$ *Haukadal Biskupstungum, 801 Selfoss, tel: 480 6800.* This hotel's large dining room gets very busy in summer with tour groups. It offers an excellent menu in the evening and a buffet at midday, including soups and salads. The locally caught salmon is superb, as is the bread baked underground in the traditional Icelandic fashion. Good two- and three-course specials. Try to leave room for the sumptuous desserts.

Lava Restaurant $$ *Blue Lagoon, Grindavík, tel: 420 8806.* Eat overlooking the thermal spa at this world-famous spot. The menu uses fish brought ashore at the nearby harbour, but presents it in a variety of international dishes including *bouillabaisse* and curried cod. There are also chicken and pasta dishes, hamburgers and a vegetarian menu. Best enjoyed after, rather than before, a dip in the hot waters.

EAST AND NORTHEAST

Bautinn $$ *Hafnarstræti 92, Akureyri, tel: 462 1818.* A good choice in the centre of Akureyri for burgers, pizzas, no-nonsense fry-ups and simple meat and fish dishes.

Strikið $$ *Skipagata 14, Akureyri, tel: 462 7100.* At the location of the former 'Fiddler on the Roof' restaurant. This is a good-quality restaurant in the heart of Akureyri with unsurpassed views of the fjord and mountains. Serves burgers, pizzas, meat and fish dishes.

Friðrik V $$$ *Kaupvangsstræti 6, Akureyri, tel: 461 5775.* Undoubtedly the finest place to dine in Akureyri. Owner and chef, Friðrik, trained at London's River Café and also worked in Reykjavík's Hótel Holt before opening this elegant first-floor restaurant serving creatively prepared fish dishes whilst blending the freshest Icelandic ingredients with a subtle hint of the Mediterranean.

Gamli Bærinn $ *Beside Hotel Reynihlíð, Mývatn, tel: 464 4170.* The name means 'old farm', and the building, which dates from

1912, is by the architect who designed Reykjavík's Parliament. The place is now a delightful little restaurant and café, where fantastic char soup (char being a type of red trout) is served. There are always specials on the blackboard, and they have live jazz and local bands at the weekend.

WEST AND NORTHWEST

Búðarklettur $$ *Brákarbraut 13-15, Borgarnes, tel: 437 1600.* The Settlement Centre's restaurant serves hearty pasta, fish and meat mains. Many have a traditional slant – think smoked lamb and herring on rye bread.

Hótel Buðir Restaurant $$$ *Main Road, Buðir, tel: 435 6700.* Reopened after a devastating fire this is one of Iceland's finest hotels. Seafood and game predominate, including honey-glazed catfish with ginger, chilli and liquorice sauce, served in its ocean-side restaurant.

Hótel Flókalundur $$–$$$ *Vatnsfjörður, tel: 456 2011.* This is the only restaurant in the vicinity. Rosemary-roasted trout with butter-fried vegetables, roast lamb and garlic lobster are some of the evening meals served. Also a popular coffee stop. Closed in winter.

Hótel Núpur $$–$$$ *Dýrafjörður, Þingeyri district* *Tel: 456 8235.* A small, but select evening menu is served in summer. Fish takes pride of place, along with the restaurant's speciality, goat meat.

Café Riis $$ *Hafnarbraut 39, Holmavík, tel: 451 3567.* A tasteful café/bar/restaurant with pizzas, burgers, freshly caught fish, and Icelandic dishes such as puffin breast with blueberries or smoked lumpfish.

Við Pollinn $$–$$$ *Hótel Ísafjörður, Silfurtorg 2, Ísafjörður, tel: 456 3360.* The most upmarket place in town to eat, with excellent fish dishes and superb views of the fjord.

A–Z TRAVEL TIPS

A Summary of Practical Information

A

ACCOMMODATION (See also CAMPING, YOUTH HOSTELS, and the list of Recommended Hotels on page 135)

The Icelandic Tourist Board (www.visiticeland.com) has recently introduced a classification system for accommodation, but not all hotels have signed up to it. The system grades hotels from five stars, for those with the best facilities, down to one star, for the most basic.

Both in Reykjavík and elsewhere in the country many of the higher-rated hotels are large and impersonal. The capital has some quality hotels with character, and there are one or two elsewhere in the country, but these are the exception. The smaller, family-run Icelandic hotels can be quite spartan and all Icelandic buildings have thin walls. In summer 13 of Iceland's schools, universities and conference centres open as 'summer hotels' (www.hoteledda.is). If you are doing a lot of walking or horse riding check if the hotel has a sauna, hot-tub or pool, all of which will be geothermally heated.

There are guesthouses everywhere in Iceland and these are generally welcoming and considerably cheaper than hotels. They vary in quality, but are invariably clean and well-kept. Bathrooms are very often shared. Farmhouse accommodation is also available. More than 130 farms operate through Icelandic Farm Holidays (tel: 570 2700, www.farmholidays.is).

If you are travelling around, the location of a hotel will probably be more important to you than its facilities. Local tourist offices *(see page 133)* have comprehensive lists of nearby hotels and staff who can speak English and make reservations for you. If you are travelling between May and September you are advised to book ahead.

AIRPORTS

All international flights arrive at **Keflavík Airport** (tel: 425 6000; www.keflavikairport.com), 50km (31 miles) from Reykjavík. After every flight arrival the Flybus transfer coach transports passengers to the BSÍ bus terminal about 1.5km (1 mile) from the centre of Reykjavík. The journey takes about 45 minutes and costs ISK1,950: buy tickets from the ticket machine or ticket booth next to the airport exit. If you require an onward minibus connection from the BSÍ bus terminal to your Reykjavík hotel, the extended journey costs ISK2,500. Taxis from the airport to central Reykjavík will take 30–45 minutes and will cost approximately ISK7,500–9,000.

Reykjavík's Domestic Airport (tel: 570 3030) is at the other end of the runway from the Loftleiðir hotel and there are regular buses to and from the city centre. **Air Iceland** (tel: 570 3030; www.airiceland.is) offers scheduled services to most parts of the country.

B

BICYCLE HIRE

Some places around Iceland hire out bikes; make enquiries at tourist offices, hotels and campsites. Cycling is popular around Lake Mývatn: Hotel Reynihlíð and the Hlíð and Bjarg campsites have a reasonable selection. **Reykjavík Bike Tours**, 101 Reykjavík, tel: 694 8956, http://icelandbike.com have rental and tours.

BUDGETING FOR YOUR TRIP

Following the 2008 financial crisis and the devaluing of the króna, Iceland is much cheaper for foreign visitors.

Getting to Iceland. The main airline serving Iceland is Icelandair, operating from both Europe and North America. In summer it is essential to book well in advance to secure the lowest fares. In the UK, Icelandair have fares from London Heathrow, Manchester and Glasgow from £190 return. Investigate special packages and offers on www.icelandair.co.uk. If you are flying from the US you can expect to pay from $600 for a return ticket.

Accommodation. Top prices in Reykjavík are over ISK50,000 for a twin room in a luxury hotel, with en-suite shower or bath, and breakfast included. Guesthouses charge around ISK12,000. In some places you pay about half the price if you use your own sleeping-bag.

Meals. A sit-down lunch in a restaurant costs from ISK1,500 (but look out for cheap lunchtime buffet deals), and dinner from ISK2,500. Alcohol is expensive, with a glass of beer costing around ISK700 and a bottle of wine upwards of ISK1,000. It's a good idea to bring your maximum duty-free allowance with you from home.

Local transport. Reykjavík's city bus service is good value, with bus tickets costing ISK280. Taxis are costly – the meter starts running as soon as the vehicle pulls up to your hotel, and a trip from Reykjavík to the international airport costs around ISK14,000 (compared to the Flybus ticket price of ISK1,950). There are various passes available from the bus company BSÍ (tel: 591 1011, www.bsi.is) and these will entitle you to discounts on ferries and at some campsites, too.

Generally, if you visit during the summer, stay in decent hotels, eat out in restaurants most nights and undertake a few activities, you should expect to pay upwards of ISK25,000 per person per day, based on two people sharing. However, it is possible to cut costs by staying in guesthouses or youth hostels and eating the odd meal in a restaurant – for this, you should reckon on about ISK10,000–15,000 per day. Camping and self-catering will cost around ISK4,000 per day.

Domestic flights are generally cheaper than buses. The same journey from the capital to Akureyri costs from ISK4,900 single. So-called "net offers" are available on most Air Iceland flights which, when booked in advance, help to secure the best price for any particular flight.

Incidentals. A sightseeing tour of Reykjavík costs ISK2,800 per person, and a half-day tour to Gullfoss and Geysir is ISK4,800. Whale-watching costs from ISK4,000. Car hire costs a minimum of ISK6,000 per day, with limited mileage. A spa treatment will cost from ISK8,500. Entrance to nightclubs is at least ISK1,200. A coffee is ISK280 – more in fashionable venues, a cinema ticket costs ISK1,000, and an Icelandic knitted jumper will cost from ISK8,000.

C

CAMPING

There are around 130 registered campsites in Iceland, although you can camp almost anywhere if you get the landowners' permission. Within national parks and conservation areas, camping is only allowed at designated spots. Official campsites are found in most towns and villages, at national parks, conservation areas, places of natural beauty and some farms and community centres. The standard varies. Expect to pay ISK900 per person per night for a layer of pumice and an earth closet to soft turf and hot showers. The recognised sites are open from June to August or mid-September.

The Iceland Tourist Board (www.visiticeland.com) has camping listings on its website. Equipment can be hired from Útilíf, Kringlan shopping centre, Reykjavík (tel: 545 1500).

CAR HIRE (See also DRIVING and BUDGETING FOR YOUR TRIP)

Several major international rental companies are represented in Iceland, as well as locally based firms. Prices are high. You must be at least 20 years old to hire a car in Iceland. Insurance is compulsory and not always included in the quoted price, so check first.

The following companies offer a full range of vehicles: Hertz (tel: 522 4400; www.hertz.is), Europcar (tel: 565 3800), Avis (tel: 591 4000; www.avis.is), ALP (tel: 562 6060; www.alp.is). Many hire companies offer one-way rentals, allowing you to drive from Reykjavík to Akureyri, for example, and then return by air.

It is worthwhile going over your intended route with the rental company to check what roads are allowed for your type of vehicle. Note that insurance companies will not cover hire cars taken into the interior.

CLIMATE

Influenced by the warm Gulf Stream and prevailing southwesterly winds, Iceland's temperate oceanic climate is surprisingly mild for the latitude. However, summers are generally cool, and the country is often wet and windy, with the weather changing dramatically from day to day as well as within one day itself. Basically, it's sensible to be prepared for all eventualities. The weather is drier and sunnier in the north and east than the south and west, although no less windy. The south coast is notoriously wet.

You can get weather information in English by calling tel: 522 6000 or visiting www.vedur.is/english.

Average rainfall and temperatures:

	J	F	M	A	M	J	J	A	S	O	N	D
°C min	-2	-2	-1	1	4	7	9	8	6	3	0	-2
°C max	2	3	4	6	10	12	14	14	11	7	4	2
Rainfall mm	76	72	82	58	44	50	52	62	66	85	72	79

CLOTHING

In summer, light woollens or a fleece, and a wind- and rainproof jacket or coat are essential, along with something for warmer days (wearing layers works best in Iceland's changeable summer weather). Take plenty of jumpers to keep you warm plus thick walking socks (and thinner ones to go against your skin).

Icelanders are very clothes-conscious, which is reflected in Reykjavík's fashion shops. If you plan to eat out at one of the city's better restaurants, you should dress up. Although most pubs are casual, people do get dressed up to go to smarter bars, and a few clubs maintain a policy of no jeans or trainers.

Pack a swimming costume, as geothermal bathing pools are very much a part of the Icelandic social scene.

CRIME AND SAFETY (See also EMERGENCIES and POLICE)

Iceland is an extremely peaceful and law-abiding nation. Of the few people in prison most are drugs offenders. Public places are well lit. Violent crime is virtually non-existent, bar the odd domestic dispute and drunken brawl. The latter is most likely on Friday and Saturday nights, when the city's youth takes to the streets of central Reykjavík on a (mostly good-humoured) drunken spree.

CUSTOMS AND ENTRY REQUIREMENTS

Iceland is a signatory to the Schengen Agreement, so, in principle, residents of other Schengen countries (Norway plus all EU countries except Britain and Ireland) can travel without document checks. Flights from the UK go through passport control. Iceland doesn't require visas from citizens of EU states, the US, Canada, Australia or New Zealand; South African citizens do require one. The normal entry stamp in your passport is valid for a stay of up to three months, and your passport must be valid for a further three months beyond your proposed departure date. There are no currency restrictions.

D

DRIVING

Despite the high cost of car hire, rental may provide the only way to see everything you wish in the time available. Driving in Iceland can also be a real pleasure – the roads are not busy and the freedom to stop to admire the scenery or go for a walk is a huge bonus. Be prepared for journeys to take a lot longer than you might expect from the distances involved.

Road conditions. While much of the main highway encircling the country is surfaced, many routes in Iceland are just gravel or unmade and full of potholes. Some roads are prone to flooding, and bridges are often single-lane.

Sandstorms can be a hazard along the coast and in some parts of the interior. In winter, snow and ice are common, and studded snow tyres are essential. For information on road conditions call tel: 1777 or check on www.vegag.is.

Rules and regulations. Icelanders drive on the right. The speed limit is 50kmh (30mph) in urban areas, 80kmh (50mph) on gravel roads in rural areas and 90kmh (55mph) on asphalt roads out of the towns.

Driving off roads is illegal, seat belts are compulsory in the front and back of a car, and headlights must be used at all times, day and night. Drink-driving, which is defined as 0.05 percent blood-alcohol content, is taken very seriously by the authorities. Offenders lose their licences and face heavy fines.

Fuel. In Reykjavík most filling stations stay open until 11.30pm. Many have automatic pumps that take credit cards after that time. Around the ring road there are filling stations every 50km (30 miles) or so, but if in doubt fill up before you move on. Prices vary, but petrol will cost approximately ISK185 per litre.

Parking. Reykjavík has plenty of parking meters, ticket machines and car parks, some of which are covered and attended. On-street parking can be hard to find. Elsewhere in the country you will encounter few problems, and there are large free car parks at most of the major tourist sites.

Road signs. The usual international symbols are used on road signs, but look out also for:

Einbreið brú	Single-lane bridge (often marked by flashing orange lights)
Malbik endar	Unmade road
Blindhæð	Blind summit

Help and information. Tourist boards have leaflets about driving on unmade roads and in winter, as well as lists of all road signs. You

can also contact Félag Íslenskra Bifreiðaeigenda (Icelandic Auto-
mobile Association, 105 Reykjavík; tel: 414 9999, www.fib.is).

E

ELECTRICITY

The electric current in Iceland is 220 volts, 50 HZ AC. Plugs are
round pin with two or three prongs.

EMBASSIES/CONSULATES

Australia: Australian Embassy in Copenhagen, Denmark, tel: (+45)
70 26 36 76, www.denmark.embassy.gov.au
Canada: Túngata 14, 101 Reykjavík, tel: 575 6500, www.canada.is
Ireland: Honorary Consul in Reykjavík, Mr David Thorsteinsson,
tel: 554 2355, e-mail: davidcsh@islandia.is
South Africa: Hús atvinnulifsins, Borgartún 35, Reykjavík, tel: 591
0355, email: jr@fif.is
United Kingdom: Laufásvegur 31, 101 Reykjavík, tel: 550 5100,
http://ukiniceland.fco.gov.uk
United States: Laufásvegur 21, 101 Reykjavík, tel: 562 9100,
http://iceland.usembassy.gov

The Icelandic Foreign Ministry has a full list of diplomatic rep-
resentatives on its website: www.utanrikisraduneyti.is.

EMERGENCIES (See also HEALTH AND MEDICAL CARE on page 119)

To contact the police, ambulance, fire service or other emergeny situations, tel: **112**.

In case of serious illness or accidents, there is a 24-hour casual-
ty department in Fossvogur; tel: 543 2000.

Chemists are signed *Apótek*, and there is at least one in every
town. Lyfja, Lágmúli 5, Reykjavík (tel: 533 2300) is open daily from
7am–1am.

In case of dental emergencies, tel: 575 0505.

G

GAY AND LESBIAN TRAVELLERS

Iceland has a tolerant attitude towards gays and lesbians. It has the world's first openly gay prime minister, and passed a gender-neutral marriage bill in 2010.

For information and advice contact: The Gay and Lesbian Association/Samtökin '78, 4th Floor, Laugavegur 3, 101 Reykjavík, tel: 552 7878, e-mail: office@samtokin78.is; www.samtokin78.is. Open daily 1.30–5.30pm; Monday and Thursday evenings there is a library and a coffee bar, open 8–11pm.

There is an annual Gay Pride celebration in Reykjavík every August, www.this.is/gaypride. More information about the gay scene in Iceland can be found at www.gayice.is.

GETTING THERE (See also Airports and Budgeting)

The fastest and cheapest way to get to Iceland is by air. **Icelandair** (www.icelandair.co.uk/www.icelandair.com) is the main airline serving Iceland, operating from both Europe and North America. In the UK, Icelandair serves London Heathrow, Manchester and Glasgow. In North America; Boston, Halifax, Minneapolis, New York, Orlando, Seattle and Toronto.

Iceland Express (www.icelandexpress.com) currently the only budget airline operating flights to Iceland, has daily year-round departures from London Gatwick and several departures weekly from London Stansted. The airline also flies to New York and Winnipeg, and to a further 15 European destinations. It operates direct flights between Copenhagen and Akureyri in northern Iceland from June to August.

The Faroese company, **Smyril Line** www.smyril-line.com, operates a ferry service to Iceland between April and September. The ship *Norrøna* sails from Esbjerg or Hanstholm in Denmark to Seyðisfjörður in eastern Iceland, calling in at Tórshavn (Faroe Islands).

GUIDES AND TOURS (See also PUBLIC TRANSPORT)

One of the best ways of seeing the main sites is by organised coach tours. The drivers and tour leaders are always well informed and speak English. If you want to travel into the interior or on to glaciers, a tour is often the only choice.

Tours are well run, and many allow you to do some exploring by yourself. **Iceland Excursions (Gray Line)**, Hafnarstræti 20, 101 Reykjavík, tel: 540 131 organise day tours from Reykjavík to the west and southwest of the country, including whale-watching, the Blue Lagoon and glacier tours.

Tours can last from half a day to three weeks. As well as sightseeing there are tours specialising in hiking, geology, birdwatching, fishing and horse riding. Sports-orientated tours have good-quality equipment and guides who are fully trained for the environment. Note that many tours do not operate in 'winter' (generally September to May). For full details, contact the Icelandic Tourist Office (www.visiticeland.com).

H

HEALTH AND MEDICAL CARE (See also EMERGENCIES)

Thanks to its clean air and low pollution, Iceland is an extremely healthy place. The water is clean to drink, although you should never drink from glacial rivers or streams. No vaccinations are required to visit Iceland. The standard of medical care is very high in Iceland, but nonetheless, all visitors should have adequate medical insurance, though an agreement exists between Iceland, the UK and Scandinavian countries for limited health insurance coverage of its residents. Travellers from those countries should obtain the European Health Insurance Card (EHIC) before leaving home.

Despite the high latitude, the Icelandic sun can still burn, especially when reflected off snow and ice. Sunblock and good sunglasses should be worn if you are outside for long periods.

In extreme circumstances hypothermia is a possibility. Symptoms include shivering, numbness, dizzy spells and confused behaviour. If affected, take shelter, remove and replace wet clothing, and consume hot drinks and high-calorie food.

Every year all too many visitors are injured, sometimes very seriously, by putting feet or hands into boiling hot mud pools and springs, so take care to avoid this. If you are planning to take part in any unusual or 'dangerous' sports, make sure that these are covered by your policy.

HOLIDAYS

The following are public holidays in Iceland. Note that most businesses, banks and shops will be closed on these days, and public transport will be more limited than usual.

Fixed dates:

1 January	New Year's Day
1 May	Labour Day
17 June	National Day
24 December	Christmas Eve (from noon)
25 December	Christmas Day
26 December	Boxing Day
31 December	New Year's Eve (from noon)

Movable dates:

Maundy Thursday
Good Friday
Easter Sunday
Easter Monday
First day of summer
Ascension Day
Whit Sunday
Whit Monday
Bank Holiday Monday (first Monday in August)

L

LANGUAGE

Icelandic is a Germanic language and has barely changed since Viking times. Although it is grammatically complex, anyone who speaks one of the other Scandinavian languages or German will recognise words and features. Thankfully, though, there is no need to master Icelandic to enjoy a holiday in Iceland, since nearly all Icelanders speak excellent English, particularly the young. The Icelandic section of the *Berlitz Scandinavian Phrase Book and Dictionary* covers most situations you are likely to encounter.

yes	**já**
no	**nei**
hello/hi	**halló/hæ**
good morning/afternoon	**góðan dáginn**
good evening	**gott kvöld**
good night	**góða nótt**
goodbye	**bless**
How do you do?	**Sæll (to a man);**
	sæl (to a woman)
Fine, thanks.	**Mél líður vel, takk.**
thank you	**takk fyrir**
yesterday/today/tomorrow	**í gær/í dag/á morgun**
Where/when/how?	**Hvar/hvenær/hvernig?**
How long/how far?	**Hvað lengi/hversu langt?**
left/right	**vinstri/hægri**
hot/cold	**heitt/kalt**
old/new	**gamalt/ungt**
open/closed	**opið/lokað**
vacant/occupied	**laus/upptekinn**
early/late	**snemma/seint**

M

MAPS

Good maps are essential to explore Iceland properly, and there are a large number available. Tourist offices have leaflets with basic maps and also sell more detailed ones. The best maps are those produced by the Icelandic National Land Survey, *Landmælingar Íslands*. This company publishes a 1:500,000 road map of the whole country as well as a series of nine 1:250,000 sheets covering all regions – these regional maps are detailed enough for hiking. The 1:500,000 touring map Ferðakort Ísland (www.ferdakort.is) is excellent, as is the 1:200,000 Ferðakort Ísland Vegaatlas (Road Atlas).

MEDIA

There are English-language newspapers and magazines on sale in Reykjavík one or two days after publication. They can also be found in public libraries *(bókasafn)*.

The magazine *Iceland Review* (www.icelandreview.com) is published in English with informative articles and great photographs. The *Reykjavík Grapevine* is an irreverent, free English-language newspaper containing articles, reviews and listings, and is available wherever there are tourists.

The government-owned Sjónvarpið and the commercial channel Skjár 1 are the two main TV channels in Iceland. Many hotels offer satellite TV giving direct access to international news and entertainment channels including CNN and the BBC.

MONEY (See also BUDGETING FOR YOUR TRIP)

The Icelandic currency is the króna (ISK; plural: krónur), divided into 100 aurar. Notes are in denominations of ISK5,000, 2,000, 1,000 and 500, coins in denominations of ISK100, 50, 10, 5 and 1. **Currency Exchange.** Banks will change foreign currency or travellers' cheques – US dollars, sterling and euros are all easily exchanged. Outside normal banking hours you can exchange money at major hotels. There are 24-hour exchange facilities available at Keflavík Airport: look for **Landsbankinn** in the arrival hall for arriving passengers; on the second level for departing passengers.

At the time of going to press, the rate of exchange was as follows: £1 = ISK181; €1 = ISK152; $1 = ISK116.

Credit Cards. Credit cards are used everywhere in Iceland, with the most ubiquitous being Visa and MasterCard/ EuroCard. American Express, JCB and Diners are far less common.

Cash advances are available on Visa and MasterCard/EuroCard from all banks, savings banks and automatic cash machines.

ATMs. The simplest way to obtain Icelandic króna is from an ATM cash machine – plentiful in Reykjavík and other Icelandic towns. There are cash machines at the airport and at many banks. The charges will depend on your bank, but the rate of exchange is generally better than any other method.

Travellers Cheques. Hotels will exchange travellers' cheques and banknotes for guests, at a rate slightly below the bank rate, depending on the availability of cash in the till.

OPENING TIMES

Shops, banks and other services rarely close for lunch. The following are rough guides to opening times in Reykjavík; opening times elsewhere in the country are usually shorter than this.

Banks: Mon–Fri 9.15am–4pm.

Post Offices: Mon–Fri 9am–4.30pm.

Shops: Mon–Sat 9am–6pm. Smaller shops may not open until 10am. Supermarkets open Sun 10am–2 or 6pm.

Liquor Stores. Reykjavík: Mon–Thur 11am–6pm, Fri 11am–7pr Sat 11am–2pm. Other stores vary from place to place, though u ally much shorter hours.

P

POLICE *(Lögregla)*

In such a law-abiding country the police keep a low profile, and you are unlikely to come across them unless you commit a motoring offence. They can normally speak some English.

Police Emergency Number, tel: **112**.

Reykjavík Police Headquarters is at Hverfisgata 113–115, tel: 444 1000. The Reykjavík city-centre police station is at Tryggvagata 19, tel: 569 9025. For lost property, contact the police headquarters (tel: 444 1000; open Mon–Fri 8.15am–4pm).

POST OFFICES *(Íslandpóstur)*

The Icelandic postal service is efficient, and there are post offices (Mon–Fri 9am–4.30pm) in every town. The Central Post Office on Pósthússtræti 5 (near Laugardalur) in Reykjavík is open Monday–Friday 9am–6pm, June, July and August Saturday 10am–2pm.

It takes up to six days for post to reach Europe or North America and 10 days for Australia, New Zealand and South Africa.

Letters are sent by either priority (A) or economy (B) service, but delivery time abroad is not noticeably different between the two services. Air-mail letters or postcards to Europe cost ISK165 (A) or ISK140 (B); to other areas they are ISK220 (A) or ISK155 (B). There are up-to-date prices and information at www.postur.is.

PUBLIC TRANSPORT

Buses. There is an excellent system of buses both in Reykjavík (run by the Reykjavík bus company Strætó) and across the country. In the capital there are two terminals for the yellow city buses, one near the harbour at Lækjartorg, at the junction of Lækjargata and Austurstræti, the other at Hlemmur, at the far end of the main shopping street, Laugavegur. Maps showing all the routes are available terminals and tourist offices.

Services run Mon–Fri, 7am–midnight, and Sun 10am–midnight. There is a flat fare of ISK280, which must be paid in exact change as you board. If you are changing buses ask for a *skiftimiði*, which is valid on all buses for 45–60 minutes. The Reykjavík Welcome Card *(see p.30)* offers you free unlimited travel for 24, 48 or 72 hours.

Long-distance buses operate from the BSÍ Coach Terminal, Vatnsmýrarvegur (tel: 562 1011, www.bsi.is). There are a variety of 'bus passports' available if you are going to use the bus network extensively, and they come with different time limits.

Taxis. Taxis are available in all the major towns and cost about ISK1,200 for 3km. There are ranks in Reykjavík on Lækjargata and Eiríksgata. To order a cab by phone call: Borgarbílastöðin, tel: 552 2440; BSR, tel: 561 0000; or Hreyfill-Bæjarleiðir, tel: 588 5522.

Flights. Air Iceland is the biggest domestic carrier, running flights to the larger towns throughout the country (tel: 570 3030, www.airiceland.is). An Air Iceland Pass with four, five or six sectors valid for 30 days, and a Fly As You Please Pass, allowing 12 days unlimited travel on domestic flights, can only be purchased before you enter Iceland. For price details tel: 570 3000.

Ferries. Herjólfur runs ferries to the Westman Islands (tel: 525 7700, www.herjolfur.is). Sæferðir (Smiðjustígur 3, tel: 433 2254, www.seatours.is) runs whale-watching tours, as well as operating fjord trips and other excursions. *Sæfari* sails from Dalvík to Grímsey (via Hrisey) in the summer (Landflutningar-Samskip, Ranarbraut 2b, 620 Dalvík, tel: 458 8970, www.landflutningar.is/saefari.

Train Travel. There are no trains on Iceland.

R

RELIGION

Just under 79 percent of Icelanders belong to the Evangelical Lutheran Church, about 3 percent are Roman Catholics, 4 percent are atheists, and various denominations account for 14 percent.

Reykjavík has a number of churches that hold regular services on Sundays and in the week. Churches in central Reykjavík include: Hallgrímskirkja, Skólavörðuholt, tel: 510 1000; Dómkirkjan (the cathedral), Kirkjustræti 16, tel: 520 9700; Landakotskirkja (Catholic cathedral), and Hávallagata, tel: 552 5388 (celebrates Holy Mass in English on Sundays at 6pm).

T

TELEPHONES

The code for Iceland is +354, followed by a seven-digit number. There are no area codes. To call abroad from Iceland, dial 00, plus the country code.

Payphones are found in post offices, filling (petrol) stations and on the street. These take coins or phone cards, which can be bought at post offices in various denominations.

There are four GSM operators in Iceland, Siminn, Vodafone, TAL and Nova. Pre-paid cards can be bought at filling stations.

Useful numbers are as follows:

114: international directory enquiries
115: international operator
118: national directory assistance

TIME ZONE

Iceland is on GMT all year round. Time in summer is as below.

Los Angeles	Chicago	New York	**Iceland**	London	Sydney
5am	7am	8am	**noon**	1pm	10pm

TIPPING

Service is always included in the bill, so tipping is not normally required. It is not usual to tip taxi drivers.

TOILETS

Public toilets are a rarity. It is better to make use of the facilities at your accommodation or at a bar or café. There is only one in Reykjavík, close to the tourist office at the junction of Bankastræti and Lækjargata.

TOURIST INFORMATION

The tourist information structure in Iceland is a little complex. The Icelandic Tourist Board (Lækjargata 3, Reykjavík, tel: 535 5500, www.visiticeland.com), promotes Iceland abroad. The regional Tourist Information Centres are separately run, and some parts of the country also have Marketing Agencies. All the various offices offer more information than you could possibly need. Staff speak excellent English and are usually very helpful. Opening times vary, but in summer they open early and close around 7pm.

The Tourist Information Centre in Reykjavík is at Aðalstræti 2, tel: 590 1550, www.visitreykjavik.is (June–mid-Sept daily 8.30am–7pm, mid-Sept–May Mon–Fri 9am–6pm, Sat 9am–4pm, Sun 9am–2pm)

In Akureyri, the Tourist Information Centre is at Hafnarstræti 82, tel: 553 5999, www.eyjafjordur.is.

In the US, contact the Icelandic Tourist Office, 655 Third Avenue, New York, NY 10017, tel: 212 885 9700, www.goiceland.org. There are currently no Icelandic Tourist Offices in Australia, Canada, Ireland, New Zealand, South Africa or the UK. Information can be obtained worldwide from www.visiticeland.com.

WEBSITES AND INTERNET ACCESS

Websites. Every business and organisation, large and small, now seems to have a website. The following listing *(overleaf)* helps to provide useful information before you arrive:

www.east.is

www.north.is

www.south.is

www.west.is

www.westfjords.is

www.visitreykjavik.is

www.icelandvisitor.com extensive tourist information website also offering online booking of tours and activities

www.vedur.is the latest weather in Iceland

www.icewhale.is Húsavík Whale Centre

www.whatson.is details of events

www.bluelagoon.is information on the Blue Lagoon

www.norvol.hi.is volcanoes in Iceland

www.bsi.is Icelandic bus times

www.skyr.is all you need to know about this delicious and extremely healthy yoghurt-style product that Icelanders rave about

Internet Access. Most cafés and bars in Reykjavík have Wi-fi, so if you are travelling with your own laptop, you can access the web for the price of a coffee.

Y

YOUTH HOSTELS

Hostelling International (Borgartún 6, 105 Reykjavík, tel: 575 6700, e-mail: info@hostel.is; www.hostel.is) has 36 excellent hostels from which to choose. These are very popular and fill up quickly, so always book ahead. The association can provide a booklet listing hostels (download it from their website) and the facilities they offer – most hostels have two- to six-bed rooms and family rooms. Duvets and pillows are complimentary. You can use your own sleeping-bag/linen or hire what you need from the hostel. A single bed in a dormitory will cost ISK3,300. Good deals on car hire and excursions are also offered by the association.

Recommended Hotels

The range of hotel and hostel accommodation in Iceland is very wide indeed. In Reykjavík there are some very stylish, world-class hotels – with prices to match. Elsewhere in the country, with one or two exceptions, there are few hotels of real character, but what is lacking in terms of ambience is usually more than compensated by a stunning location. At the top end of the market, most hotels are fairly standard airport-style establishments. There is a reasonable selection of smaller, family-run hotels and guesthouses throughout the country, as well as budget accommodation for backpackers and hikers. Some schools double up as tourist accommodation during the holidays and this can be a very economical option.

High season is usually from the beginning of May until the beginning of September, when prices often double, and rooms can be hard to come by. You can often find good discounts with early online bookings. From the end of September some places close altogether, although you should be able to find a room in most towns. The bigger hotels are increasingly offering special activities, such as snowmobiling, to attract visitors out of season.

There is no publication that covers accommodation for the country as a whole, but some organisations such as Hostelling International (www.hostel.is) and Icelandic Farm Holidays (www.farmholidays.is) publish annual brochures listing details of their accommodations. Links can also be found on the website of the Icelandic Tourist Board (www.visiticeland.com).

The price guidelines below are for a double room with bathroom in high season, including breakfast and tax, unless otherwise stated. Hotels usually accept payment by credit card, but payment for guesthouses, farms, hostels and camp sites is generally by cash only. For making reservations, Iceland's country code is 354 (there are no local codes in Iceland).

$$$$	over USK25,000
$$$	USK19,000–25,000
$$	USK12,000–18,000
$	below USK12,000

REYKJAVÍK

Centerhotel Arnarhvoll $$$$ *Ingólfsstræti 1, tel: 595 8540, www. centerhotels.is.* One of the city's newest hotels, Arnarhvoll is cool, clean, and has stunning views across the bay. Five minutes' walk from the bar-and-restaurant action on Laugavegur.

Hótel Borg $$$$ *Pósthússtræti 11, tel: 551 1440, www.hotel borg.is.* This imposing building close to the Parliament was the city's first hotel. Beautifully renovated in modern style, with nods to its Art Deco heritage.

Hótel Cabin $$ *Borgartún 32, tel: 511 6030, www.hotelcabin.is.* Hótel Cabin is located a little out of the centre but upper-storey rooms have terrific views over the bay. Standard rooms are very small, but they are great value for Reykjavík.

Hótel Holt $$$$ *Bergstaðastræti 37, tel: 552 5700, www.holt.is.* This hotel is very elegant and comfortable, with great character and style. The public areas are an art-lover's delight, with the largest private collection of Icelandic paintings in existence. The rooms are well equipped, if a little small, and the restaurant is superb. It is also well known for having one of the finest ranges of whiskies in the country.

CenterHotel Klöpp $$$$ *Klapparstigur 26, tel: 595 8520, www. centerhotels.is.* Located right in the centre of town, this hotel has a cool, minimalist style, with lots of slate, wooden decor, large windows and brightly decorated bedrooms. A breakfast buffet is served between 7–10am, but there is no restaurant. The nearby Centerhotel Skjaldbreið (Laugavegur 16, tel: 595 8510) is run by the same company.

Hótel Leifur Eríksson $$$ *Skólavörðustígur 45, tel: 562 0800, www.hotelleifur.is.* The hotel has a prime location right opposite the Hallgrímskirkja church. This is a friendly family-run place with basic but comfortable rooms and a snack bar serving light meals and drinks 24 hours a day.

Luna Hotel Apartments *Spítalastígur 1, tel: 511 2800, www. luna.is.* Restored 1920s town house in a quiet central part of town, with tasteful and stylish apartments. Studio apartment ISK14,900 per night, large two-room apartment ISK38,500.

Óðinsvé $$$$ *Oðinstorg 11, tel: 511 6200, www.hotelodinsve.is.* The pleasant, relaxed atmosphere make this hotel, in a quiet residential quarter close to the centre, a comfortable place to stay. All rooms have tasteful Scandinavian decor, but deluxe rooms with split levels are the business.

Radisson Blu 1919 Hotel $$$$ *Pósthússtræti 2, tel: 599 1000, www.radissonblu.com/1919hotel-reykjavik.* Housed in the elegant former headquarters of the Eimskip shipping company, this hotel offers style and elegance right in the heart of the city and is one of the most sought-after addresses in which to stay. Old-fashioned charm meets Nordic chic.

Hótel Reykjavík Centrum $$$$ *Aðalstræti 16, tel: 514 6000, www.hotelcentrum.is.* Built above Reykjavík's oldest (Viking) house, there is nothing archaic about this airy modern hotel. Comfortable rooms with the city on the doorstep.

Reykjavík Downtown Youth Hostel $$ *Vesturgata 17, tel: 553 8120, e-mail: reykjavikdowntown@hostel.is.* Hostelling International Iceland opened a second Reykjavík hostel in 2009. This smart addition is central, with sunny staff, spacious rooms, free Wi-fi and a clean, green ethical stance.

Room with a View $ *Laugavegur 18, tel: 552 7262, www.room withaview.is.* For a good, cost-effective alternative to a hotel, try these luxurious apartments on the main shopping street. A kitchen and steambath are available to guests, and the balconies offer impressive views.

Salvation Army Guesthouse $ *Kirkjustræti 2, tel: 561 3203, email: guesthouse@guesthouse.is.* The cheapest guesthouse in Reykjaví There are no frills but this hostel-style place is neat and clean a the central location is excellent. Single, double and triple rooms, and sleeping bag accommodation. There are facilities for cooking on the ground floor.

Three Sisters Guesthouse $$ *Ránargata 16, tel: 565 2181, www. threesisters.is.* A splendid alternative to a hotel room, these cosy studio apartments near the harbour come with bedrooms and kitchenettes.

SOUTH AND SOUTHEAST

Árnanes Country Hotel $$ *Airport Road, Höfn, tel: 478 1550, www.arnanes.is.* Here you'll find farm-stay accommodation with 15 rooms, all run by a local artist, whose paintings are on display in the gallery restaurant. The rooms are spacious and comfortable, with a lovely rural feel.

Hótel Eldhestar $$$ *Vellir, 810 Hveragerði, tel: 480 4800, www.hoteleldhestar.is.* As well as offering riding tours, Eldhestar horse farm has a lovely one-storey wooden eco-hotel attached. Rooms are comfortable, with direct access to the garden, and there are log fires in the communal areas. There is full disabled access.

Hótel Geysir $$$ *Haukadal Biskupstungum, 801 Selfoss, tel: 480 6800, www.geysircenter.is.* Located right next to the world-famous geysers, this is a friendly, family-run establishment and gets very busy with tour groups in high season. There are hot tubs (accessible in summer only) and an outdoor pool. Horse-riding and quad-bike tours offered.

Hótel Hlíð $$$ *Krókur (between Hveragerði and Þorlákshöfn), tel: 483 5444, fax: 562 4001, www.hotel-hlid.is.* This is an ideal hotel for exploring the Hveragerði region and the Westman Islands. All 21 rooms have have their own facilities and are fitted with internet connections.

⸱eiðrið Guesthouse $ *Faxastígur 33, Heimaey, Westman Islands, ⸱481 1045, www.tourist.eyjar.is.* Very good value for money and staying here feels like being taken into an Icelander's home. Offers sleeping bag accommodation. Bicycles available for hire.

Hótel Hvolsvöllur $$$ *Hlídarvegur 7, 860 Hvolsvöllur, tel: 487 8050, www.hotelhvolsvollur.is.* Comfortable small hotel near the Saga Centre, handy for the new ferry service to the Westman Islands.

Hótel Klaustur $$$ *Klausturvegur 6, Kirkjubæjarklaustur, tel: 487 4900, www.icehotels.is.* Icelandair has built this large modern hotel in a town with literally one street, but it's very welcome as there is nothing else to this standard for some distance around. Out of season you could find you have the whole place to yourself. The friendly and helpful staff are always welcoming.

Hótel Lundi $ *Víkurbraut 26, Vík, tel: 487 1212, fax: 487 1404, www.hotelpuffin.is.* A delightful little place with a cosy dining room and bar. Lundi means puffin in Icelandic, and the owners, who are great nature enthusiasts, will be more than happy to tell you where to go and see the real things.

Hótel Þórshamar $$-$$$ *Vestmannabraut 28, Heimaey, Westman Islands, tel: 481 2900, www.hotelvestmannaeyjar.is.* A fairly upmarket hotel with a lower-priced guesthouse attached. A jacuzzi and sauna await you after a busy day sightseeing

Fosshotel Vatnajökull $$$$ *781 Hornafjörður, tel: 478 2555, www.fosshotel.is.* Situated outside the town, this hotel is well located for jeep tours on to the glacier.

EAST AND NORTHEAST

Gistihúsið Egilsstöðum $$ *Egilsstaðir, tel: 471 1114, www. egilsstadir.com.* This converted stone farmhouse aims to recreate the atmosphere of early 20th-century rural Iceland. The building dates from 1903, and its parlour and collection of period artefa all add to the effect. It's just west of the town on the shores of I Lagarfljót. There are horses in the paddock.

Fjarðahótel $$$ *Búðareyri 6, Reyðarfjörður, tel: 474 1600, www.fjardhotel.is.* This bright and airy hotel is on the main road through the village. Rooms are plain and simple, yet comfortable. The town makes a good alternative to Egilsstaðir for exploring the Eastfjords.

Hótel Hérað $$$ *Miðvangur 5, Egilsstaðir, tel: 471 1500, www.icehotels.is.* Part of the Icelandair chain, this smart newly renovated hotel is a welcome sight after a long day hiking.

Fosshotel Húsavík $$$ *Ketilsbraut 22, Húsavík, tel: 464 1220, www.fosshotel.is.* Probably the world's only whale-themed hotel. The staff can organise whale-watching trips for you, and there is a welcoming bar to help you warm up on your return, as well as a good restaurant.

Hótel Kea $$$$ *Hafnarstræti 87–9, Akureyri, tel: 460 2000, www.hotelkea.is.* A reliable and comfortable hotel in Akureyri, close to all the town's restaurants and shops. The rooms have mini-bars and satellite television, and there is free internet access in the lobby.

Hótel Mývatn $$$ *Skútustaðir, 660 Mývatn, tel: 464 4164, www.myvatn.is.* A modern, if rather austere, three-storey building with magnificent views over the lake. Staff will help to organise tours throughout the year. The Skútustaðir pseudocraters are just a few minutes walk away.

Hótel Norðurland $$$ *Geislagata 7, tel: 462 2600, fax: 462 7962, www.keahotels.is.* Located right in the heart of Akureyri, this pleasant hotel with 24 en-suite double rooms is another in the KEA chain and makes a good economical choice. Downstairs there's an in-house restaurant with a good choice of main meals, including pizzas. Perfect location for exploring the town centre.

Hótel Reynihlíð $$$$ *Reynihlíð, 660 Reykjahlíð, tel: 464 4170, www.reynihlid.is.* This family-run hotel has been extended many times to accommodate the growing number of tourists to the Lake Mývatn area. The newer rooms are smart and modern, and there is a lovely little café and bar in the adjoining Old Farm building that can get very lively in the evenings. It's important to book well ahead in high season. The hotel also offers sleeping-bag accommodation.

Gamla Gistihúsið $ *Mánagata 5, 400 Ísafjörður, tel: 456 4146, www.gistihus.is.* A sweet-and-sunny guesthouse in the middle of the Old Town, with shared bathrooms. Also has sleepingbag accommodation.

Hamar Youth Hostel $ *Borgarbraut 9, 310 Borgarnes, tel: 695 3366, email: borgarnes@hostel.is.* Set in a beautiful farmhouse at the golf club northeast of Borgarnes, with views over nearby Borgarfjörður and the Skarðsheiði mountains.

Hótel Ísafjörður $$-$$$ *Silfurtorg 2, 400 Ísafjörður, tel: 456 4111, www.hotelisafjordur.is.* Right in the town centre. Standard rooms are average; it's worth paying extra for deluxe. The highlight is the good restaurant with its fine fjord views. The owners also run the summer-only Edda Hotel.

Fosshótel Reykholt $$$ *Reykholt, tel: 435 1260, www.fosshotel.is.* Surrounded by rolling countryside and enjoying one of the most historic locations in western Iceland, this hotel is perfectly placed for visiting the former home of saga writer Snorri Sturluson. Redesigned and reopened as a cultural themed hotel based on Norse mythology, pictures and features throughout the hotel act as reminders of Iceland's stirring medieval literary history.

Hótel Tindastóll $$$ *Lindargata 3, Sauðárkrókur, tel: 453 5002, www.hoteltindastoll.com.* Built in 1884, the Hótel Tindastóll is not only the oldest hotel in Iceland but also one of the nicest and most unusual. With its stone walls and timber beams it retains a great sense of history. The original front door is still intact, and there all kinds of antique artefacts dotted throughout. Every room good size with modern amenities. Marlene Dietrich stayed while entertaining the troops during World War II.

INDEX

Berlitz® pocket guide

Iceland

Second Edition 2011

Written by Lance Price and James Proctor
Series Editor: Tom Stainer

No part of this book may be reproduced, stored in a retrieval system or transmitted in any form or means electronic, mechanical, photocopying, recording or otherwise, without prior written permission from Berlitz Publishing. Brief text quotations with use of photographs are exempted for book review purposes only.

Photography credits
All pictures APA Ming Tang Evans except:
Courtesy Blue Lagoon 3ML, 39; Icelandic Tourist Board/www.bluelagoon.is 8; Icelandic Tourist Board/Randall Hyman 36, 88, 92; Icelandic Tourist Board /Ingi Gunnar Jóhansson 96; Icelandic Tourist Board/Ruth Gundahl Madsen 61; Icelandic Tourist Board/Frederic Reglain 89; Icelandic Tourist Board/Dieter Schwitzer 50, 84; Icelandic Tourist Board/Ragnar Th. Sigurðsson 3TR
Istockphoto 2BR, 47, 49; APA Britta Jaschinski 96, 97, 101; APA Lance Price 18, 21, 46, 79, 81, 83, 95
Cover picture: AWL Images

Every effort has been made to provide accurate information in this publication, but changes are inevitable. The publisher cannot be responsible for any resulting loss, inconvenience or injury.

Contact us

At Berlitz we strive to keep our guides as accurate and up to date as possible, but if you find anything that has changed, or if you have any suggestions on ways to improve this guide, then we would be delighted to hear from you.

Berlitz Publishing, PO Box 7910, London SE1 1WE, England.
email: berlitz@apaguide.co.uk
www.berlitzpublishing.com